$8^{\underline{00}}$

MOUNTAINBIKE!
NORTHWEST WASHINGTON

N

MOUNTAINBIKE!
NORTHWEST WASHINGTON

A GUIDE TO TRAILS & ADVENTURE

JOHNZILLY

SASQUATCH BOOKS
SEATTLE

Acknowledgments

To everyone who helped me on this book with encouraging words, inspiring ideas, critiques, food, trail suggestions, love, and patience at my guidebook-writing ways—thank you so much. It is not hyperbole to say that I would not have completed this book without all of your help, right down to the last Jolly Rancher offered and accepted 23 miles into an epic. I'd especially like to thank Steve DeBroux for his research assistance and all those excellent stories, and Angela Castañeda for her love and support.

Printed in the United States of America.
Distributed in Canada by Raincoast Books Ltd.
02 01 00 99 98   5 4 3 2 1

Cover and interior design and composition: Kate Basart
Cover photograph: John P. Kelly/The Image Bank
Research assistance: Steve DeBroux
Interior photographs: John Zilly, Steve DeBroux, Wade Praeger, Greg Strong, Lisa Strong

Library of Congress Cataloging in Publication Data
Zilly, John.
    Mountain bike! northwest Washington : a guide to trails and adventure
/ John Zilly.
            p.   cm.
        ISBN 1-57061-138-6
            1. All terrain cycling—Washington (State)—Guidebooks. 2. Bicycle trails—
    Washington (State)—Guidebooks. 3. Washington (State)—Guidebooks. I. Title.
GV1045.5.W2Z44 1998
917.97'70443—dc21   98-16759

SASQUATCH BOOKS
615 Second Avenue
Seattle, Washington 98104
(206) 467-4300
books@SasquatchBooks.com
http://www.SasquatchBooks.com

Sasquatch Books publishes high-quality adult nonfiction and children's books related to the Northwest (Alaska to San Francisco). For more information about our titles, contact us at the address above, or view our site on the World Wide Web.

Northwest Washington

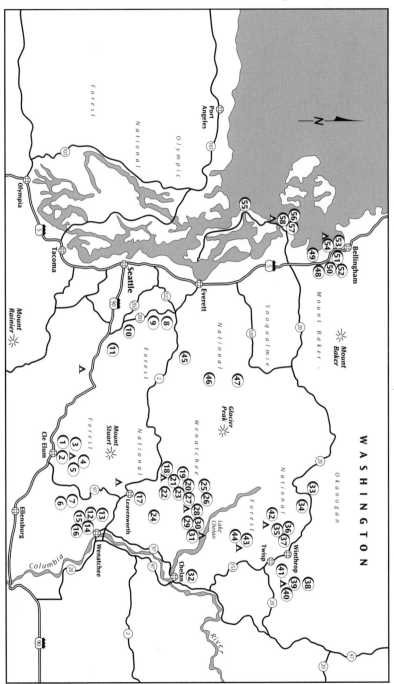

Contents

CENTRAL WASHINGTON CASCADES & FOOTHILLS

NORTHEASTERN CASCADES

NORTHERN LOWLANDS & FOOTHILLS

Rides by Difficulty, Season, Views

EASY ✺

Ride №	Ride Name	Spring	Summer	Fall	Winter	Views
9	Tolt Pipeline Trail	●	●	●	●	
36	Yellow Jacket Trail		●	●		
51	Lake Padden	●	●	●	●	
54	Interurban Trail	●	●	●	●	

INTERMEDIATE ✺✺

Ride №	Ride Name	Spring	Summer	Fall	Winter	Views
2	Coal Mines Trail	●	●	●		
10	Snoqualmie Valley Trail	●	●	●	●	
25	Entiat River		◐	●		●
32	Echo Ridge		●	●		●
41	Pipestone Canyon		●	●		
46	Monte Cristo Townsite		●	●		

DIFFICULT ✺✺✺

Ride №	Ride Name	Spring	Summer	Fall	Winter	Views
1	Roslyn Slickrock		●	●		●
4	Iron Creek		●	●		
6	Table Mountain		●	●		
8	Cherry Creek	●	●	●	●	
11	CCC Road	●	●	●		
13	Red Hill		●	●		
16	Pipeline Trail		●	●		
17	Freund Creek		●	●		
19	Chikamin Creek		◐	●		
21	Minnow Ridge		●	●		
22	Lower Chiwawa Trail		●	●		
23	Mad Lake		◐	●		●
24	Lower Mad River Trail		◐	●		
26	North Fork Entiat River		●	●		
31	Darby Draw		●	●		
33	Cutthroat Lake		◐	●		●
35	Rader Creek		●	●		

Ride Nº	Ride Name	Spring	Summer	Fall	Winter	Views
37	Black Bear Trail		●	●		
39	Lightning Creek		●	●		
40	Bear Mountain		●	●		
42	Twisp River Trail		●	●		
45	Wallace Falls	◐	●	●		●
47	White Chuck Bench	◐	●	●		
48	Squires Lake	●	●	●		
49	Blanchard Hill	●	●	●		
52	Upper Lake Padden	◐	●	●		
53	Chuckanut Mountain	●	●	●	●	●
55	Fort Ebey State Park	●	●	●		
56	Heart Lake	●	●	●		
57	Anacortes Community Forest	●	●	●		
58	Whistle Lake	●	●	●		

MORE DIFFICULT ✺✺✺

Ride Nº	Ride Name	Spring	Summer	Fall	Winter	Views
3	West Fork Teanaway River		◐	●		
7	Naneum Creek		●	●		
14	Devils Gulch		●	●		
15	Mission Ridge		●	●		●
18	Nason Ridge		◐	●		●
27	Klone Peak		◐	●		●
28	Lake Creek		◐	●		●
30	Twenty-Five Mile Creek		◐	●		●
34	Cedar Creek		●	●		
38	Starvation Mountain		◐	●		●
43	Eagle Lakes		◐	●		●
50	Lookout Mountain	●	●	●		●

EXTREME EPIC ✺✺✺✺

Ride Nº	Ride Name	Spring	Summer	Fall	Winter	Views
5	Miller Peak Epic		●	●		●
12	Little Camas Creek Epic		●	●		●
20	Chikamin Ridge Epic		◐	●		●
29	Pot Peak Epic		◐	●		●
44	Foggy Dew Epic		◐	●		●

About the Author

John Zilly is the Northwest's very own mountain biking guru. In 1980, fresh out of high school, he spent nine months circumnavigating the United States by bike, surviving 57 flats and pedaling more than 10,500 miles. After also touring Europe from the saddle, he exchanged his thin tires for fat ones and has been exploring the dirt trails of the Northwest ever since. He is the author of six mountain biking guidebooks, including the best-selling *Kissing the Trail*, a guide to rides near Seattle, and *Mountain Bike! Southwest Washington*, the companion to this volume. John researches all the routes himself and creates his maps using GPS tracking data. John lives in Seattle with his wife, Angela.

Riding a Good Story

I was burnt. I straddled my bike in the middle of the dirt road and stared at the map, squinting and furrowing at the lines and dots—a nasty bout of map-face. A big drip of sweat fell from my nose and was absorbed between topographic lines. By any measure, it was a beautiful day in the Wenatchee Mountains. But I was tired and hot, and after sixteen straight days of riding, I wished for a day off from biking in the mountains.

I had pedaled up a series of gated dirt roads in search of Lower Red Hill Trail, rumored one of the best singletrack descents on the planet. But numerous old roads mazed through the area, making it difficult to find the route. Now the main road forked left and climbed a steep, sun-exposed hillside toward Red Hill. The lesser fork to the right—a faint old doubletrack—didn't appear on the map, though it held the promise of following the creek. Another drip of sweat hit the map.

I put the map away and looked for a moment at the creek folding over itself and darting away. This was supposed to be recreation, re-creation. The goal wasn't just to research a guidebook or bomb down a killer descent, it was to use the elements of mountain biking to re-create myself, to return to my campsite in some sense a new person. I turned right and glided along the doubletrack, following the creek. After a few hundred yards it abruptly ended and an unmarked singletrack continued.

The narrow singletrack meandered and then wound up the hillside away from the creek. After a mile, I began a grueling, switchbacking ascent and, over the next forty-five minutes, burned a birthday cake worth of calories. Hot sun filtered through the fir forest. I still had no idea what to expect of this trail, where it would go or when it would end. After three steep miles, the trail ended at a dirt road. I pulled out the map again and realized that I might be able to create a new loop—an epic. Fig Newtons in hand, I felt full of the spirit of adventure and discovery. I chided myself for having allowed mountain biking to become routine and predictable.

Late in the day I reached Upper Red Hill Trail, a trail I wouldn't have known if I had compassed the loop planned that morning. I launched down the steep descent, whipping around a set of furious switchbacks. The velvety trail leveled and cruised the wide spine of Red Hill. A short distance farther, the trail skirted an unusual series of smooth rock escarpments that jutted up like giant eggs to form an edge along the top of the ridge. To the east of the rocks, a long, curving talus cliff dropped a thousand feet into Devils Gulch. I peered through the rocky gaps. The cliffs and the light and the cool late afternoon air seemed to relax time.

As I stood at the edge of the cliffs looking down into Devils Gulch, I remembered that a friend had told me, "There's always a story on a good ride." Perceived chores and predictable descents were just obstacles to getting there. I hope *Mountain Bike! Northwest Washington* inspires you to go out and make your own great stories.

Choosing a Ride

You ought to be able to easily and efficiently select a ride, get to the trailhead, and then negotiate the route (for epic rides, all bets are off). That should be the guiding principle, so to speak. It's my hope that *Mountain Bike! Northwest Washington* functions that way for you. The following describes the rating system, explains how the information is presented, and provides an annotated look at some of the wording conventions I use to detail each ride.

Difficulty Rating

The difficulty rating is measured in wheels, ranging from one to five, with one wheel being easiest and five wheels being hardest. The difficulty rating is based on the length of the trip, the hill factor and elevation gain, and the level of bike-handling skill required. This quick reference is located near the title of each ride.

(easy): Just about anyone can accomplish a ride rated as one wheel; it isn't much different from riding on a paved country road. These rides are short and flat, and have well-packed riding surfaces. One-wheel rides stick to wide, smooth dirt roads or rail-trails.

(intermediate): Two-wheel rides primarily traverse dirt roads and rail-trails, although they occasionally venture onto easily negotiated doubletrack and singletrack for short stretches. These rides are somewhat longer and may have more elevation gain than those rated one wheel. These routes never demand a high skill level, and riders will rarely hike-a-bike.

(difficult): More rides in this book receive this rating than any other. These routes—all of which contain some singletrack—travel less than 20 miles and have moderate elevation gains, generally less than 1,600 feet. Typically, a ride rated three wheels combines a dirt-road climb with a singletrack descent. Be prepared for at least a few steep climbs as well as some technical sections of trail that may require hike-a-biking.

(most difficult): If a ride is long, hilly, and chock-full of challenging singletrack, I have rated it four wheels. Some riders may have to push or carry their bikes for long distances. You'll gain big chunks of elevation and have your bike-handling skills tested on every four wheeler. Remember: If you're not hiking, you're not mountain biking.

(extreme epic): Three rides in this book are sufficiently difficult to warrant an extreme, epic rating of five wheels. These rides are very long, technical, hilly, and, at times, dangerous, usually requiring miles of walking or hike-a-biking as well as complex route-finding. Do not attempt them unless you are an expert mountain bicyclist, in great physical condition, and enjoy pushing yourself to the limit.

Ride Statistics

Distance
This information is given in miles.

Ride
I have noted the format of each route here, either Loop or Out & Back, as well as the types of trails and roads the route traverses. On some rides, the word **views** appears on this line. Of course every ride has *some* view, but if a ride is marked as a views ride, then on clear days you should expect to see a snow-capped volcano, a spectacular mountain lake, a panoramic vista, or all of the above.

Duration
The duration of a ride depends on your skill, stamina, and map-reading abilities, as well as what you did the previous night. Trail conditions and weather can also drastically alter the time it takes to complete a ride. Before you leave, call to find out about current trail and weather conditions.

Travel time
Estimated driving times are listed, usually from the nearest two major cities.

Hill factor
"How hard are the hills?" is often the first question cyclists ask about a given route. This quick reference describes the difficulty of the climbs. The elevation gain, measured from the ride's low point to high point, is also listed. (By the way, singletrack climbs that average more than 300 feet per mile and road climbs that average more than 450 feet per mile are very difficult.)

Skill level
Rides are rated for beginner, intermediate, advanced, or expert, depending on the minimum bike-handling ability a rider should have before attempting a particular trail. This rating has nothing to do with fitness; you may be a fine athlete, but I wouldn't recommend an expert trail if you have never mountain biked before.

Season
This entry lists the best time of year to be out on this trail. Seasonal trail closures are also noted. Call the managing agency for current trail conditions and restrictions.

Maps
Supplementary maps are key, unless you enjoy bivouacking. I typically recommend United States Geological Survey (USGS) topographical maps, United States Forest Service district maps, Green Trails maps, or Washington State Forest maps.

Users
This entry notes what types of users are likely to be out on the trail.

More info
Here the agency that manages each trail is named, and its phone number is provided. For current trail conditions, maintenance schedule, snow level, permit information, and other restrictions, call ahead.

Prelude

Each ride begins with a descriptive overview, which paints a landscape and recounts trail anecdotes.

To Get There

This paragraph provides detailed instructions for driving to the trailhead. In most cases, I have indicated a point at which you should set the trip odometer in your car to zero.

The Ride

In addition to notes about the terrain and landscape, and an occasional quip, the ride section contains a detailed description of the route—up or down, left or right. These paragraphs note the mileage—in bold—for most intersections, hills, tricky sections of trail, vistas, and other significant landmarks. Riding with an odometer is highly recommended.

What follows is an annotated listing of some of the conventions I use in describing the trails in *Mountain Bike! Northwest Washington*. **WHOA!** signifies a dangerous section of trail or a turn easily missed, and warns the rider to pay close attention. **Stay on the main trail/road** means that other trails or roads exit from the main trail—use good judgment to continue on the primary trail or road. When the trail dead-ends at another trail, forcing a 90-degree turn either right or left, the resulting three-way intersection is described as a **T**. Other three-way intersections are usually described as **forks**, though sometimes I write that the **trail divides**. If a faint trail **(lesser trail)** forks off the main trail, I will sometimes tell you to **ignore** it or **pass** it rather than describe it as a fork. When two trails or roads cross, the result is usually referred to as a **four-way intersection**. On many trails you'll have to **walk** or **push** your bike up a steep hill. If, however, a long stretch of trail requires an awkward combination of walking and riding, I describe it as a **hike-a-bike**. A **technical** section of trail—typically a narrow tread or steep slope populated by roots, rocks, or other obstacles—demands good bike-handling skills. On unmaintained trails or on trails transformed by clearcutting and road building, it's sometimes difficult to figure out which way to go. In these instances, I'll likely mention the problematic **route-finding**.

There are a number of different types of trails and roads described in this book. A dirt or gravel **road** could be used by a car. Roads in national forests are usually identified by a number preceded by **FR** for Forest Road. **Doubletracks**, also know as **jeep trails, jeep tracks**, or **old roads**, refer to narrow, rough roads and may be either motorized or nonmotorized. Often, these old roads are **gated** to keep out motor vehicles. Old railroad grades, or **rail-trails**, are abandoned railroad lines that have no tracks or ties. Typically, rail-trails have the look and feel of dirt roads, except that rail-trails are usually flat and nonmotorized. **Trail** and **singletrack**, terms that are used interchangeably, generally refer to soft-surface trails less than 36 inches wide. A **wide trail** refers to a path 3 to 8 feet wide. Sometimes, however, "trail" is used in a generic sense to mean any part of a route, whether paved or soft-surface, between 12 inches and 12 feet wide.

Option

For some rides, I have provided directions to modify the route. Occasionally the option shortens the trip, but in most cases it adds mileage and difficulty, often to bag a peak or catch a nice view.

Gazetteer

Each ride concludes with information on nearby campgrounds and services. The information on the nearest town helps pinpoint the ride's location, or at least lets you know which direction to head to satisfy that Iced Animal Cookie craving. Use the information noted under the Gazetteer heading to plan weekend trips. Often several rides start from the same trailhead or can be accessed from the same campground.

The Maps and GPS Features

I recorded the route, mileage, and elevation data using a Global Positioning System (GPS) receiver, a cycle computer, and an altimeter. Using these tools, I created maps for *Mountain Bike! Northwest Washington* that have a lot of cool features.

The most unique feature of the maps is certainly the GPS data. Using a network of space-based satellites, GPS receivers monitor and track latitude and longitude. I recorded the twists and turns of every route, then used that track data to create the maps. In some cases, the maps in *Mountain Bike!* are more accurate than any existing map. (Keep in mind, though, that recreational GPS receivers have a small error factor.) In addition to recording the track data, I used the receiver to make a series of waypoints (GPS lingo for an exact location) for each ride, which I call Ridepoints. Individual Ridepoints are marked by numbered triangles at key junctures along the ride; you'll also find a complete list of Ridepoints—a route—for each ride in a small box on the map.

The Ridepoint numbers are latitude and longitude coordinates (WGS 84 map datum). Ridepoint 1 is the trailhead. To use the Ridepoints, punch the coordinates into your GPS receiver the night before a ride. The following day, your receiver will point toward each successive Ridepoint for the entire loop.

Additional map features: The start and finish of each ride is clearly visible, and the highlighted route prevents map face—squinted eyes and a furrowed brow. Arrows indicate the direction of travel, and intermediary mileages are noted between the triangular Ridepoints. The small graphs tell the basic elevation story of each ride, and key elevations are noted along the route.

Safety: Keep the Rubber Side Down

At the top of a particularly long, ear-popping descent, a friend turned to me and said, "Have fun and keep the rubber side down." He smiled, and pedaled away. The smile on his face indicated he was having fun. As for his second piece of advice, well, let's just say he didn't heed it. For historical accuracy: When we finished the downhill he didn't say, "You've got to try that skin-side-down technique sometime." Humorous, except for the fact that losing skin is perhaps one of the least painful scenarios.

Though it's probably more dangerous to drive to the trailhead, bicycling injuries such as cracked collarbones, dislocated shoulders, fractured wrists, and broken heads are all too common. True, no matter how much care you take, the occasional header is inevitable. If lucky, you'll be able to hop up and shake it off, but if you've sustained serious injuries, extra clothes and a first-aid kit can save your life.

Of course, the danger of mountain biking isn't just the spectacular crash. A simple mechanical failure, a sore knee, a wrong turn, or exhaustion can strand you miles from the trailhead and force an unplanned night in the woods. If you don't have the proper supplies and a friend to plan strategy with, you could be in trouble. Ironically, the worst trouble is often self-inflicted: It originates out of panic and hysteria. If you can stay calm, if you have enough to eat and drink, and if you have an extra layer of clothing to put on, you will probably be fine no matter how dire the situation seems.

Before You Leave

- How's the trail? Is it hunting season? Call the managing agency.
- Call the National Weather Service, 206-526-6087.
- Let someone know where you plan to ride.

During the Ride

- Never ride alone.
- Always wear a helmet.
- Wear eye protection.
- Avoid excessive speed. Ride as if a small child is around every corner.
- Carry a first-aid kit.
- Carry extra clothes and a hat, no matter how nice the weather seems.
- Pack sunscreen, a lighter, a pocket knife, extra food, and a flashlight.
- Drink at least two quarts of water per day. Don't count on finding water.
- Carry a map of the area and bring a compass.
- Use a cycle computer.

Recommended Tools

- pump
- patch kit
- extra tube
- tire irons

- spoke wrench
- chain tool
- Allen wrenches
- needle-nose pliers

- crescent wrench
- screwdriver
- spare brake cable

Live on Earth: The Trail-Use Debate

I recently had an eye-opening conversation with a local Sierra Club leader about the Middle Fork of the Snoqualmie River Trail near North Bend, Washington. The Middle Fork Trail—beautiful and wild, through old growth along the river—was the only singletrack in the North Bend Ranger District that was open to bicycles. The rangers there had been managing the trail as open to bicycles since it was rebuilt (using multi-use money, by the way) in 1992. However, after several years of pestering, the Sierra Club managed to goad the Forest Service into closing the Middle Fork Trail to bikes. I asked this Sierra Clubber why they had done that, why it had been necessary to close the last trail in the district to bikes, especially when bicyclists were the primary users. He said that since the trail hadn't been hardened with concrete pavers, it wasn't appropriate for bikes. Hikers, he said, didn't want to walk through any mud on their winter outings along the Middle Fork.

Clearly, he didn't know the first thing about bicycles or trails. No one advocates building nonmotorized trails with concrete pavers. And the newest scientific studies (*Erosional Impact of Hikers, Horses, Motorcycles, and Off-Road Bicycles on Mountain Trails in Montana*, Wilson and Seney, 1994) show that hikers and mountain bikers have about the same erosional effect on trails, even in wet conditions. So his boots are going to get muddy even without bikes on the trail.

But I'm not out to get into a who-does-more-damage argument, or even blast the Sierra Club. I'm a member myself, and I believe in much of what we have accomplished over the years. In fact, more than 65 percent of mountain bicyclists consider themselves environmentalists. Call me radical, but with hundreds of trails open for hiking in the North Bend Ranger District, it seems unreasonable to close the last section of singletrack open to bicycles because some guy doesn't like to get mud on his boots when he goes hiking in February. That's not "environmental," that's selfish recreational elitism. The local Sierra Club chapter should work on improving the environment rather than alienating a big group of environmentalists over a short section of trail.

The real issue behind recreational elitism is often overcrowding. Indeed, some trails are overcrowded, but if you are willing to drive a little farther to the trailhead, you'll find that many trails aren't overcrowded, even on August weekends. This area is growing fast, and all recreationalists—even hikers—need to tailor their expectations. If you do choose to use a trail that's convenient and popular, then it's absurd to have great expectations of a solitary meditation out on the trail. And if you want to hike in February on a soft-surface trail in western Washington, plan to get your boots dirty.

Our Responsibility

Like all trail users, we need to take responsibility for the way we behave out on the trails. If we adversely affect the environment or frighten other trail users, then we shouldn't be there. Out-of-control speed freaks who skid down the trail or scare other users have no rights to the trail.

Most bicyclists, however, search out the magic that's hidden around each bend in the trail—the mossy old growth, the spawning salmon. We can't deny that mountain biking is great fun. And why should we? Being out in nature should be a joyous, not solemn, occasion. Just remember that you can be joyous without abusing the trail or the other users on it.

Cyclists have been a central part of the conservation movement for years—commuting, vacationing, and doing errands on bicycles. Bicyclists have been building and sharing soft-surface trails in western Washington for more than 100 years. In fact, bicyclists helped invent the idea of wilderness recreation. For that good tradition to continue, we need to keep searching for that magic, yielding the path to others, riding gently, and helping to maintain trails. Also, be aware that state and federal user fees are coming. Many national forests already require a permit to park at trailheads.

The Rules

- Don't leave any trace.
- Don't skid—ever. Take it easy on poorly constructed trails, and avoid wet trails or trails liable to be marred by tires. Walk around all delicate areas.
- Respect all other trail users. Yield the right of way to everyone, including hikers, runners, other bicyclists, motorcyclists, and equestrians.
- Stop and dismount when you encounter horses. Stand on the downhill side of the trail, and talk to the horse and rider as they pass.
- Always ride in control.
- Respect wildlife (you are in their home!) and livestock.

The Land You Are On

Most of the rides in *Mountain Bike! Northwest Washington* traverse trails and roads on public land. But idiosyncratic trails don't always adhere to ownership boundaries, and many trails cross in and out of private timber land or development tracts. Ownership can change at any time, so if you run into a "No Trespassing" sign, it's time to turn around. In addition, timber harvests on public and private land can decimate trails. Even without the problem of clearcuts, the money pinch on public lands leaves some trails unmaintained. So for many reasons, get in the habit of calling the land manager before heading out.

Land managers don't always like hearing from us, but if they know that mountain bikes account for a large percentage of the use on a trail, they'll have a harder time closing it. Hearing from users and constituents makes a difference. Land managers make major decisions based on public input. Be a squeaky wheel.

Land Managers

Land Managers

Anacortes Parks and Recreation	360-293-1918
Bellingham Parks and Recreation	360-676-6985
King County Parks	206-296-4232
Mount Baker-Snoqualmie National Forest	206-775-9702
National Forest Service	206-220-7450
National Park Service	206-220-7450
Okanogan National Forest	509-826-3275
Skagit County Parks	360-336-9414
Washington State Department of Fish and Wildlife	360-902-2200
Washington State Department of Natural Resources (DNR)	800-527-3305
Washington State Parks	800-233-0321
Wenatchee National Forest	509-662-4335
Whatcom County Parks	360-733-2900

Political Offices

United States House of Representatives	202-224-3121
United States Senate	202-224-3121
Washington State Legislative Switchboard	800-321-2808
White House Switchboard	202-456-1414

Clubs

Backcountry Bicycle Trails Club (Seattle)	206-283-2995
Cascade Bicycle Club (Seattle)	206-522-2407
International Mountain Bike Association (IMBA)	303-545-9011
Single Track Mind (Tacoma)	206-565-5124

Out Riding: Tips and Techniques

Eating

Eat constantly to avoid the dreaded double-headed bonk. Eating is more important than training and *way* more effective at holding that bonk at bay than all the titanium components your bank account can afford. I usually start out with at least 1,000 calories of food in my pack: candy bars, energy bars, peanuts, Fig Newtons, and at least one piece of fruit to avoid energy-bar stomach, from which no amount of Tums can save you.

Drinking

Always bring plenty of water and drink constantly. Two quarts a day is the minimum. I've quaffed three quarts of water on a really hot day. Eating and drinking enough can get you up a lot of hills.

Walking

Most riders will push their bikes during some part of every ride included in *Mountain Bike!* that is rated three, four, or five wheels. Walking your bike is nothing to be ashamed of—it's part of the sport. Walk to avoid getting hurt, walk to save your legs for the rest of the ride, and walk around muddy areas to save delicate trails.

Cadence

As a rule, it's best to pedal 70 to 100 rotations per minute while riding a bike. This can seem awkwardly fast if you're not used to "spinning." But a healthy cadence is the easiest way to keep your legs fresh for the longest time possible. Slow, laborious pedal strokes strain muscles, tiring them for the miles ahead. On rough trails, the cadence rule doesn't always apply, but it's good to keep in mind in order to stay smooth and loose.

Descents

The header, digger, cartwheel, and flip are bad. Riding sideways toward small children is also bad. Either ride in control or walk down the steep sections. Sit back to lower your center of gravity, and keep your arms and legs slightly bent. Keep your hands firmly and consistently on the brakes; you'll get nowhere waving one arm around like a cowboy. Don't use your front brake suddenly or erratically. The conundrum of braking: The front brake does most of the real braking, but you have more precise steering and you're less likely to take a header if less pressure is applied to the front brake. Remember that speed is the most hazardous bicycling condition—it's difficult to get hurt at 1 mile per hour; at 20 miles per hour, it's all too easy.

Climbs

The idea is to get to the top without hurling. Ride at a pace you can sustain for the length of the climb, concentrating on deep, relaxed breathing. Avoid locomotive breathing. Generally, it's best to stay seated so your rear wheel doesn't spin out. If traction is not a problem, try pedaling in a standing position occasionally to save your butt and utilize different muscles. Remember: It's okay to take a rest break.

Training

Do some. Of course, if you're already out riding, then it's too late for me to do much sermonizing, but you'll have a better time if you've put some miles in before a tough ride. More importantly, carefully select the ride or your riding partner. Don't ride an epic with an über-biker if you'd rather be following first-gear Freddy on a three-wheeler.

Maintenance

You'll have more fun out on the trail if your bike rolls smoothly, doesn't skip gears, and doesn't screech when you brake. Think about it: All week long you have to deal with copy machines that don't copy, computers that crash, and co-workers who skip gears and screech—so doesn't it make sense that when you are spending your own free time, you use something that works the way it's supposed to? Keep your bike in good working order.

1

CLE ELUM
Roslyn Slickrock
◌◌◌

Distance	17.8 miles
Ride	Loop; dirt road, jeep trail, singletrack, slickrock; views
Duration	2 to 5 hours
Travel time	Ellensburg—30 minutes; Seattle—1.5 hours
Hill factor	Road climbs, trail descents, some steep; 1,300-foot gain
Skill level	Intermediate (plus river ford)
Season	Summer, fall
Maps	Green Trails: Kachess Lake, Mount Stuart
Users	Bicyclists, equestrians, hikers
More info	Wenatchee National Forest, Cle Elum District, 509-674-4411

The pine forest near Roslyn

Prelude

Perhaps as a tribute to Moab, an uncharted singletrack leads to a huge slab of granite near Roslyn, providing one of the nicest slickrock experiences this side of southern Utah. Even at eighty-five miles per hour, the drive to Moab takes about seventeen hours, so the prudent mountain biker must allot at least four days to make the round trip and catch a few rides. Well, with this ride, you can take care of slickrock business and get home for dinner, whether you're coming from Bellingham, Seattle, or Wenatchee (Portlanders may want to spend the weekend and check out some of the fine Teanaway River or Taneum Creek rides nearby). Though much of the route travels over dirt roads, the singletrack, the slickrock, and the adventurous river ford make it a ride I will definitely return to. Two big **WHOA!** factors here: First, the edges of the big granite slab are not marked, and going off the edge would be bad. Second, the maze of unmarked trails in this area make route-finding challenging.

To Get There

A few miles west of Cle Elum on Interstate 90, take exit 80. Proceed east toward Roslyn on Bullfrog Cutoff Road. After about 2.5 miles, reach State Route 903 and turn left. Start your odometer here. After several miles, SR 903 winds through Roslyn. Stay on the main road through the town. At 7.6 miles, find Forest Road 4305 on the right. Take this road, and park immediately.

The Ride

From the junction of SR 903 and FR 4305, pedal up the forest road. The dirt road ascends through a thin pine forest. When you reach a fork at **0.5** mile, bear right and continue up. At **0.6** mile, the road divides: Turn right onto FR 113. This rough, narrow dirt road soon crosses Bear Creek, then forks at **0.9** mile: Go left. From here, FR 113 switchbacks eastward up a broad ridge, quickly gaining big chunks of elevation. Around the **3**-mile mark, the road levels and bends around to the right, revealing views of Cle Elum Lake to the west.

At a fork, **3.2** miles, take the less-traveled FR 114 on the right, and continue the climbing up the rutted, sometimes trenched, road. As you ascend, pass by numerous unmarked singletracks on the left that appear promising. Just past the crest of a hill, **4.4** miles, take an unmarked trail around to the left of a huge rock. **WHOA!** This is an easy turn to miss (if

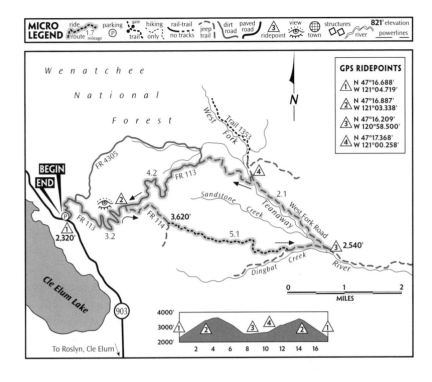

you reach a fork in the road, you've gone too far). From the big rock at the top of the hill, the trail forges a choppy way, up and down, along the ridgeline. A couple of steep pitches may force a short push. At a fork in the trail, **4.8** miles, go left. At **5.7** miles, ignore a trail back to the right.

Arrive at the big slab of slickrock at **6.3** miles. **WHOA!** While playing on the rock, which is about a quarter mile long and a hundred yards wide, watch out for the dangerous drop-offs. As the trail reaches the north side of the rock, it veers down to the right and continues descending into the Dingbat Creek drainage. (Mileages here do not include any distances ridden on the rock.) From the slickrock, the trail drops precipitously before leveling somewhat and bearing left. Ignore two trails on the left at around the **7**-mile point. At **7.4** miles, reach a T and turn left onto a dou-bletrack. At **8.1** miles, reach a second T and turn left. Stay on the main road. At **8.2** miles, cross West Fork Teanaway River, then at **8.3** miles take a hard left and begin riding up West Fork Teanaway River Road.

Stay on the main track as you ride up this old rocky road. Pass over a small washout at the **9.3**-mile mark. At **10.3** miles, ignore a spur road on the left. At **10.4** miles, however, take the lesser spur on the left that leads to the river. Ford the river, wide and shallow here, to the jeep track opposite. From the bank of the river, the road is steep and rough, but soon the grade mellows and the tread smooths out. At a fork in the road, **11** miles, bear right. At **11.6** miles, arrive at a fork and go left. When the road divides at **11.8** miles and **11.9** miles, take the right fork each time. After a short descent reach a T, **12** miles, and turn left on FR 113. The climb is easy at first, but becomes more difficult as the road switchbacks up. Ignore several trails as you climb.

Crest the top of the ridge at **14.1** miles. Coast the gradual descent to a fork at the **14.6**-mile mark to complete the lollipop top of the loop (FR 114 forks left). Continue straight on FR 113, retracing your tire tracks to the junction of FR 4305 and SR 903 to complete the loop, **17.8** miles.

Gazetteer

Nearby camping: Wish Poosh Campground (USFS), Indian Camp Campground (DNR, primitive)
Nearest food, drink, services: Roslyn

2 CLE ELUM
Coal Mines Trail
◎◎

Distance	6.4 miles
Ride	Out & Back; rough gravel and dirt rail-trail
Duration	1 hour
Travel time	Ellensburg—30 minutes; Seattle—1.5 hours
Hill factor	Slight incline, no steep hills; 360-foot gain
Skill level	Beginner
Season	Spring, summer, fall
Maps	USGS: Cle Elum
Users	Bicyclists, equestrians, hikers
More info	Cle Elum-Roslyn Chamber of Commerce, 509-674-5958

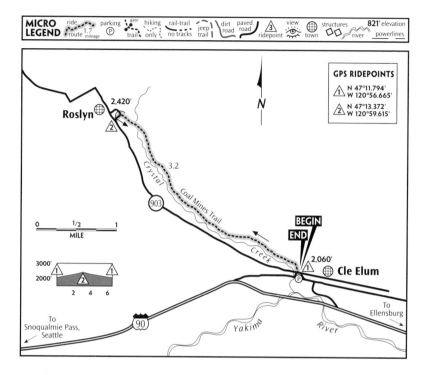

Prelude

The Coal Mines Trail, a rail-trail administered by the towns of Cle Elum and Roslyn, traces the route of a defunct railroad. In the future, it may be extended to the town of Ronald. The trailhead remains unfinished, though quite functional. Rising toward Roslyn along Crystal Creek, it is short and gently graded. But I've rated it two wheels because of the rough, uneven riding surface.

To Get There

From Seattle, take Interstate 90 eastbound to exit 84. The exit ramp becomes First Street in Cle Elum. Continue down First Street for about a mile and turn left at the sign for the Coal Mines Trail. Park immediately in the triangular gravel parking area bounded by First Street and Stafford Avenue.

The Ride

From the triangular parking area, head east, away from First Street. Almost immediately, cross Second Street West, following the Coal Mines Trail signs. Just across Second Street, the rail-trail begins, climbing gently toward Roslyn along Crystal Creek through a mixed pine forest. The wide, gravelly tread is rough and uneven. At **1.5** miles, cross a dirt road. Cross another dirt road at **2.8** miles. Soon after crossing a paved road, **3** miles, the rail-trail forks: Bear left, pedal about one block, and turn left on East Washington Avenue. At **3.2** miles, reach the intersection of East Washington Avenue and North First Street in Roslyn. After you are done exploring Roslyn, turn around and pedal back down the Coal Mines Trail to Cle Elum to complete the ride, **6.4** miles.

Gazetteer

Nearby camping: Wish Poosh Campground (USFS), Indian Camp Campground (DNR, primitive), Taneum Campground (USFS)
Nearest food, drink, services: Cle Elum

3 West Fork Teanaway River

☼☼☼☼

Distance	26.4 miles
Ride	Out & Back; singletrack, dirt road
Duration	4 to 6 hours
Travel time	Ellensburg—30 minutes; Seattle—1.5 hours
Hill Factor	Tricky trail ascent, some hike-a-bike; 2,080-foot gain
Skill level	Expert
Season	Late summer, fall
Maps	Green Trails: Kachess Lake, Mount Stuart
Users	Bicyclists, equestrians, hikers, motorcyclists
More info	Wenatchee National Forest, Cle Elum District, 509-674-4411

Prelude

The trail up West Fork of the Teanaway River has a wild and remote feeling. Basalt cliffs jut up from the fickle current that pools and flows through the narrow canyon; small pines cling to tiny ledges in the rock.

For some of the route, the trail is precariously etched into high ledges above the river, resulting in the four-wheel rating. In other sections, loose rock or compact dirt make up the trail's tread, and you'll find yourself alternating between zipping around a tight turn, pushing up a steep, rocky slope, and shouldering your bike to ford the river. In other words, it's a hard ride. I rode this trail on a bright October afternoon, when sharp reds and yellows of changing leaves popped in the receding autumn light, the river

West Fork Teanaway River canyon

pooling, then running again in the gorge below. I felt like I had been transported into a Sierra Club calendar.

To Get There

Take Interstate 90 to exit 85 near Cle Elum. From the north side of the interstate, set your odometer to zero, and bear right onto State Route

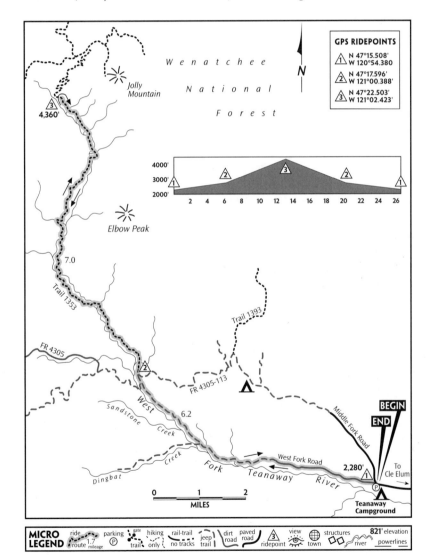

970 toward US Highway 97 and Wenatchee. At 6.5 miles, turn left on Teanaway Road. At 13.5 miles, turn left on West Fork Teanaway Road. At 14 miles, find Teanaway Campground on the left, and park.

The Ride

Ride west on West Fork Teanaway Road. At the western entrance of the campground, the road divides: Stay to the left on West Fork Teanaway Road. The road meanders along the north side of West Fork Teanaway River. Stay on the main road, ignoring spur roads on the right and left. As you proceed, the road loses its maintained feel, becoming progressively more bumpy and rocky. After passing through a gate, reach a fork at **4** miles and bear right, continuing along the north side of the river. Stay on the main track as you ride up this old rocky road. Pass over a small washout at the **5**-mile mark. At around **6** miles, ignore several spur roads. At **6.2** miles, just as the road switchbacks to the right, find a small parking area for West Fork Teanaway Trail 1353 on the left. Take the trail.

From the small parking area, ride out the old roadbed. After a few hundred yards, several large rocks block the way to vehicle traffic. The wide trail soon narrows to singletrack. At **6.7** miles, part of the trail has washed into the river, forcing a short ford. At this point, the valley has narrowed to a tight, winding canyon with the trail etched into the side.

At **8** miles, the trail crosses the river, necessitating the first real ford of the ride. From here, the trail crosses the river five more times, assuring wet feet even during low water. Though the overall elevation gain up the river valley is moderate, the trail rises and falls quickly, mandating numerous short pushes as well as longer sections of hike-a-bike for all but the strongest and most skilled riders. **WHOA!** In several places the trail bears up and away from the river, revealing dangerous exposures. At around the **13.2**-mile mark, the trail veers to the northeast, away from the river, toward Jolly Mountain and becomes quite steep. Turn around and ride back to the campground to complete the ride, **26.4** miles.

Gazetteer

Nearby camping: Wish Poosh Campground (USFS), Teanaway Campground (private)
Nearest food, drink, services: Cle Elum

CLE ELUM

4 Iron Creek

⊕⊕⊕

Distance	11.4 miles
Ride	Out & Back; singletrack
Duration	2 to 3 hours
Travel time	Ellensburg—1 hour; Wenatchee—1.5 hours; Seattle—2 hours
Hill factor	Healthy climb; 1,200-foot gain
Skill level	Intermediate
Season	Summer, fall
Maps	Green Trails: Mount Stuart, Liberty
Users	Bicyclists, equestrians, hikers, motorcyclists
More info	Wenatchee National Forest, Cle Elum District, 509-674-4411

Approaching the summit of Teanaway Ridge

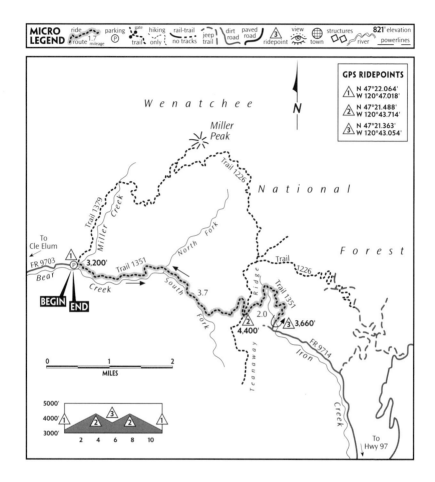

Prelude

Begin this entirely singletrack route by fording Bear Creek and meandering through a dense forest along a dark dirt trail. As the trail climbs to a saddle at Teanaway Ridge, the environment dramatically changes from plush forest on the western, Bear Creek side to parched, open hillsides on the eastern, Iron Creek slope. From the saddle, the fine-rock trail zips down the valley to Iron Creek at the far end of the Out & Back. Sections of the ride are steep and require short hike-a-bikes.

To Get There

Take Interstate 90 to exit 85 near Cle Elum. From the north side of the interstate, set your odometer to zero, and bear right onto State Route 970 toward US Highway 97 and Wenatchee. At 6.5 miles, turn left on Teanaway Road, which eventually becomes Forest Road 9737. When the road divides at 19.9 miles, bear right, continuing on FR 9737. At 21.2 miles, turn right on FR 9703. At 24.7 miles, reach the end of FR 9703 and the trailhead for Iron Bear Trail 1351.

The Ride

From the trailhead, take Iron Bear Trail 1351 and immediately ford Miller Creek. The trail winds through a dense pine and fir forest while following Bear Creek. Cross the creek numerous times over the first several miles, as you gradually ascend the valley. The trail bends right and follows South Fork of Bear Creek, becoming steeper after the **2.2**-mile mark. At **2.9** miles, the ascent gets more difficult as you climb out of the forest up the open, brushy head of the valley. This section may be a hike-a-bike for some.

At **3.7** miles, reach a four-way intersection at the top of Teanaway Ridge. Proceed straight ahead on Iron Bear Trail 1351. From the ridge top, the smooth and compact trail descends into Iron Creek, switch-backing down a wide, open slope and offering views of the trail below. At **5.7** miles, after a fast, furious descent, the trail ends at FR 9714. From here, turn around and pedal back up and over Teanaway Ridge, returning to the Iron Bear trailhead, **11.4** miles, to complete the route.

Gazetteer

Nearby camping: Beverly Campground (USFS, primitive)
Nearest food, drink, services: Cle Elum

5 Miller Peak Epic

✿✿✿✿✿

Distance	20.2 miles
Ride	Loop; singletrack, dirt road; views
Duration	3 to 7 hours
Travel time	Ellensburg—1 hour; Wenatchee—1.5 hours; Seattle—2 hours
Hill factor	Grueling climbs, lots of hike-a-bike; 2,420-foot gain
Skill level	Expert
Season	Summer, fall
Maps	Green Trails: Mount Stuart, Liberty
Users	Bicyclists, equestrians, hikers, motorcyclists
More info	Wenatchee National Forest, Cle Elum District, 509-674-4411

Views into Alpine Lakes Wilderness from east flank of Miller Peak

Prelude

This epic ride will reward you with breathtaking views of Mount Stuart and the surrounding countryside—if you're willing to do a lot of strenuous hiking. The ride took forever to complete, which didn't make any sense considering that, for a five-wheel epic, its distance is relatively short and its elevation gain squat. But the long stretches of hike-a-bike, out-and-out pushing, and steep, technical trail caused me to ditch my plans for a second ride that sunny August day. We didn't carry enough food, and when someone spilled peanuts, we all scrambled around, picking them up off the trail to eat. Toward the end, the ride loses about 1,600 feet of elevation in just two miles—a shameful waste of elevation, as one friend said.

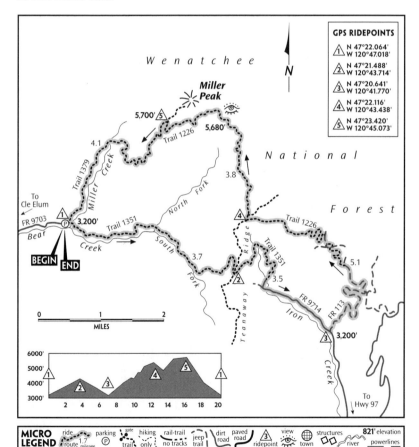

To Get There

Take Interstate 90 to exit 85 near Cle Elum. From the north side of the interstate, set your odometer to zero, and bear right onto State Route 970 toward US Highway 97 and Wenatchee. At 6.5 miles, turn left on Teanaway Road, which eventually becomes Forest Road 9737. When the road divides at 19.9 miles, bear right, continuing on FR 9737. At 21.2 miles, turn right on FR 9703. At 24.7 miles, reach the end of FR 9703 and the trailhead for Iron Bear Trail 1351.

The Ride

From the trailhead, take Iron Bear Trail 1351 and immediately ford Miller Creek. The trail winds through a dense pine and fir forest, paralleling Bear Creek. Cross the creek numerous times over the first several miles, as you gradually ascend the valley. The trail bends to the southeast and follows South Fork of Bear Creek, becoming steeper after the **2.2**-mile mark. At **2.9** miles, the ascent gets more difficult as you climb out of the forest up an open, brushy slope at the head of the valley. This section may be a hike-a-bike for some.

At **3.7** miles, reach a four-way intersection at the top of Teanaway Ridge. Proceed straight ahead on Iron Bear Trail 1351. From the ridge top, the smooth and compact trail descends toward Iron Creek, switchbacking down an open slope. At **5.7** miles, after a quick descent, the trail ends at FR 9714. Coast down the dirt road; ignore a road on the right at **5.8** miles. WHOA! After a rapid dirt-road descent, turn back to the left onto old, rutted FR 113 at **7.2** miles. Grind slowly up this rugged road, dripping buckets of calories. The grade gets steeper yet at the **8.5**-mile mark, possibly requiring a short push. But soon the way levels and traverses to a fork at **9.2** miles. Turn left and immediately begin another extremely steep climb.

After one-half mile the road levels, traverses for a short stretch, then ends at **10** miles. Views: The grand Peshastin Creek Valley spreads to the north. From the end of the road, County Line Trail 1226 begins, heading northwest up the ridge along the Chelan and Kittitas County line. Plan to walk most of the next half mile as the trail switchbacks up through a sparse pine forest. The trail traverses, then crosses a dirt road at **10.6** miles. At **10.7** miles, the trail seems to end at a dirt road: Turn right and ride up the road. Most of the next four miles is a hike-a-bike. After a short distance, bear left onto a loose, poorly built trail and push your bike to the top of a ridge, **11.2** miles. After a tricky, winding, pine-spotted ridge-top trail, reach a fork at **12.3** miles and turn right. **WHOA!** This is an easy turn to miss. Just beyond this turn, ignore a faint trail on the right.

Traversing on Trail 1226

After a short traverse and a few brushy, noodling turns, the trail drops radically to a rocky notch in the ridge below, **13.5** miles. Ride past several striking rock escarpments, then hike-a-bike up the dry, open hillside toward Miller Peak. After a long slog up the exposed hillside, the grade eases and the trail turns west, **14.7** miles. An overlook at this westward bend in the trail offers stunning views of the Stuart Range to the north. From here, the trail traverses the topographic wrinkles of the steep, barren south slopes of Miller Peak. At **16.1** miles, reach a fork in the trail. Turn left, and descend Miller Peak Trail 1379. (To bag Miller Peak, turn right and climb 700 feet in less than one-half mile, so it's probably best to leave your bike at the fork and walk it.) Over the next few miles, as rocky and steep and switchbacked as it gets, you descend back into a fir and pine forest that's a sharp contrast to the barren beauty of the east side of Teanaway Ridge. Ferns mark the path of mossy-rocked streams that trickle into Miller Creek. Watch for other users during this fast descent. The terrain levels somewhat after the **18**-mile point. At **20.2** miles, reach the trailhead to complete the loop.

Gazetteer

Nearby camping: Beverly Campground (USFS, primitive)
Nearest food, drink, services: Cle Elum

6
BLEWETT PASS
Table Mountain
☺☺☺

Distance	15.6 miles
Ride	Loop; singletrack, dirt road
Duration	2 to 5 hours
Travel time	Ellensburg—1 hour; Wenatchee—1 hour; Seattle—2 hours
Hill factor	Difficult up and down, some pushing; 1,120-foot gain
Skill level	Advanced
Season	Summer, fall
Maps	Green Trails: Liberty, Thorp
Users	Bicyclists, equestrians, hikers, motorcyclists
More info	Wenatchee National Forest, Cle Elum District, 509-674-4411

Riding across a Table Mountain meadow

Prelude

Advanced riding skills are needed on sections of this route that travels over loose, rocky, root-strewn trails and steep slopes (funny for a ride that crosses fat, plateau-topped Table Mountain). The sparse pine forest and sagebrushy meadows are lovely and the surprising rock formations interesting. Across some of the meadows, the rocky trail is faint and

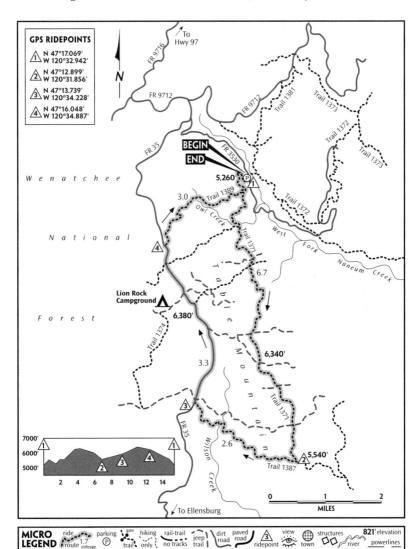

obscure: Follow the cairns and use your route-finding skills. Many trails, jeep trails, and dirt roads cross the Table Mountain–Naneum Creek area, allowing for lots of loops and exploration.

To Get There

Take Interstate 90 to exit 85 near Cle Elum. From the north side of the interstate, bear right onto State Route 970 toward US Highway 97 and Wenatchee. After about 10 miles, bear left onto US 97. Continue north on US 97 toward Wenatchee. At Blewett Pass, turn right on Forest Road 9716—start your odometer here. At 3.9 miles, go left on FR 9712. At 5.6 miles, turn right on FR 35. At 5.7 miles, turn left on FR 3530 toward Naneum Meadows. At 6.4 miles, ignore the spur road (FR 115) on the left. Continue down FR 3530 to 7.9 miles, where you'll find Naneum Meadows trailhead. Park alongside the road.

The Ride

From the trailhead on FR 3530, ride west on Trail 1389. Without allowing any time for you to warm up, the trail immediately switchbacks up a steep hill, possibly requiring a push. Reach a fork at **0.6** mile, and turn left on Naneum-Wilson Trail 1371. The trail descends, becoming successively steeper and more ragged as it nears Owl Creek. After crossing Owl Creek, reach a fork, **1.5** miles, and bear left. From here, plan to walk the next several switchbacks as you climb out of the Owl Creek ravine, up a rocky, root-strewn trail.

At **2.3** miles, cut diagonally across a dirt road to remain on Trail 1371. At **2.4** miles, ride straight through a confusing four-way: Stay on Trail 1371. Ride past some interesting rock formations and talus slopes. Cross a small stream at **2.8** miles, then head up, possibly walking, for the next quarter mile. Continue climbing, though at an easier rate, through a sparse pine forest to the **3.6**-mile point, then noodle across the northwest corner of Table Mountain. At **3.9** miles, the trail crosses a jeep trail and ascends at a gentle pace. At **4.5** miles, the trail crosses another jeep trail, then enters a meadow. Follow the cairns that mark the faint, bumpy trail, riding south across the center of this flat mountain.

Cross a dirt road at **4.9** miles. Cross another dirt road a mile farther, then descend across several bumpy, sagebrushy meadows. At **6.7** miles, reach a T as Trail 1371 ends at Trail 1387: Turn right and ride east, hanging on during the quick ups and downs of the trail. At **9.3** miles, arrive at FR 35. Turn right and pedal up the road toward Lion Rock. After a tough dirt-road climb, crest the high point of the route at **11** miles. At **11.6** miles, pass the entrance to Lion Rock Campground on the left. Gradually descend toward Naneum Meadow Trail 1389, on the right at **12.6** miles. Pedal down this fast, zippy trail toward Owl Creek. Ignore a faint trail on the right at **14.5** miles. At **15** miles, reach a fork and turn left. Drop down the trail, twisting past roots and around switchbacks, to FR 3530 to complete the loop, **15.6** miles.

Gazetteer

Nearby camping: Swauk Campground (USFS), Lion Rock Campground (USFS, primitive)
Nearest food, drink, services: Cle Elum, Leavenworth

7

BLEWETT PASS

Naneum Creek

☼❀❀❀

Distance	9.3 miles
Ride	Loop; singletrack
Duration	2 to 5 hours
Travel time	Ellensburg—1 hour; Wenatchee—1 hour; Seattle—2 hours
Hill factor	Short, steep ups and downs; 420-foot gain
Skill level	Expert
Season	Summer, fall
Maps	Green Trails: Liberty
Users	Bicyclists, equestrians, hikers, motorcyclists
More info	Wenatchee National Forest, Cle Elum District, 509-674-4411

Prelude

This trail is heavily traveled by equestrians, so remember to yield the trail to them. Generally it's best to step off the trail on the downward slope and talk to the horse and rider as they pass. When passing equestrians from behind, be sure they hear you approaching. Never zip around blind corners, because spooking a horse is dangerous and results

Haney Meadow

22

in terrible karma. Unfortunately, the heavy horse use has beat on this trail, leaving it postholed and ragged. Add a rocky soil and numerous surface roots, and the combination creates a technical challenge. Last word: Trippy basalt formations.

To Get There

Take Interstate 90 to exit 85 near Cle Elum. From the north side of the interstate, bear right onto State Route 970 toward US Highway 97 and Wenatchee. After about 10 miles, bear left onto US 97. Continue north on US 97 toward Wenatchee. At Blewett Pass, turn right on Forest Road 9716—start your odometer here. At 3.9 miles, go left on FR 9712. At 5.6

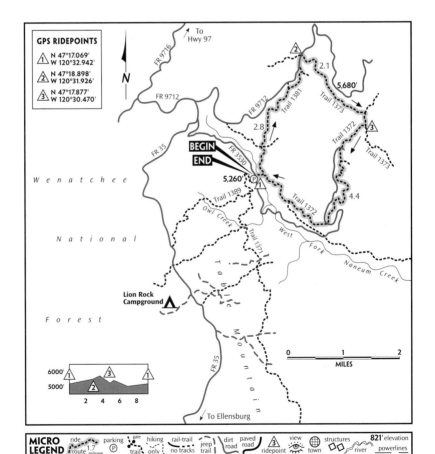

miles, turn right on FR 35. At 5.7 miles, turn left on FR 3530 toward Naneum Meadows. At 6.4 miles, ignore the spur road (FR 115) on the left. Continue down FR 3530 to 7.9 miles, where you'll find Naneum Meadows trailhead. Park alongside the road.

The Ride

From the trailhead on FR 3530, ride east on Trail 1389. Cross the West Fork of Naneum Creek, then, after **0.2** mile, reach a T and turn right on Naneum Creek Trail 1381. Due to loose rocks on the trail and ragged tread postholed by horses, all but the strongest and most skilled riders will hike-a-bike the next two miles. At **0.7** mile, ride straight through a four-way intersection, continuing on Trail 1381. From here the trail climbs, paralleling Naneum Creek. In the forests above the creek, steep climbs, roots, and postholes make for technical riding.

At **2.1** miles, reach a fork and bear right, toward Haney Meadow. At **2.5** miles, hit a fork at Haney Meadow: Bear left and scramble up to the dirt road (FR 9712). Turn right on FR 9712, pass Haney Meadow Horse Camp, then find Old Ellensburg Trail 1373 on the right, **2.8** miles. Take it. The Old Ellensburg, considerably more ridable than Naneum Creek Trail, climbs for a mile, then descends to a fork at **4.6** miles: Turn right on Howard Creek Trail 1372. At **4.9** miles, take a hard right, continuing on Trail 1372. WHOA! This is an easy turn to miss. After another stretch of hike-a-biking up a steep hillside, the thin forest opens up and affords a nice series of views to the east. Though more ridable, the trail remains rocky and uneven.

Cross a road at **6.1** miles. Reach a fork at **6.5** miles and bear right. Cross a dirt road at **7.4** miles, continuing down a sometimes smooth, sometimes rocky trail. At **8.4** miles, reach a fork and bear right on Naneum Creek Trail 1381. Enter a thicker forest, then switchback down toward Naneum Creek. Arrive at a fork, **9.1** miles, and turn left. Return to the trailhead at **9.3** miles to complete the loop.

Gazetteer

Nearby camping: Swauk Campground (USFS), Lion Rock Campground (USFS, primitive)
Nearest food, drink, services: Cle Elum, Leavenworth

8 SNOQUALMIE RIVER
Cherry Creek
⬡⬡⬡

Distance	19 miles
Ride	Loop; doubletrack, dirt road
Duration	2 to 5 hours
Travel time	Seattle—1 hour; Bellingham—2 hours
Hill factor	Several healthy dirt-road climbs; 810-foot gain
Skill level	Intermediate
Season	Year-round
Maps	USGS: Carnation, Lake Joy, Sultan, Monroe
Users	Bicyclists, equestrians, hikers
More info	Washington State Department of Natural Resources, South Puget Sound Region, 360-825-1631

Catching some air near Cherry Creek

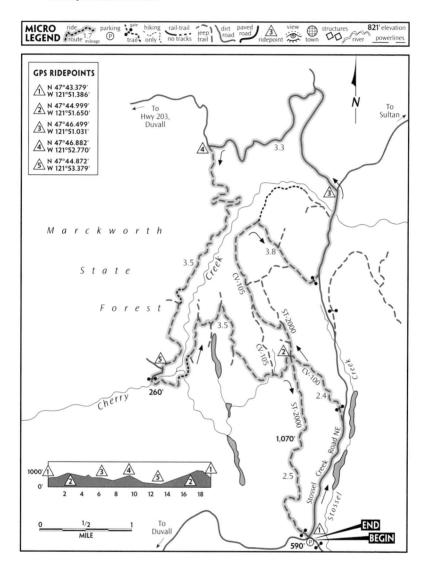

MICRO LEGEND ride route 1.7 mileage | parking ℗ | gate hiking trail | trail only | rail-trail no tracks | dirt road | paved road | jeep trail | view | 3 ridepoint | view | town | structures | river | 821' elevation | powerlines

GPS RIDEPOINTS

⚠1 N 47°43.379' W 121°51.386'

⚠2 N 47°44.999' W 121°51.650'

⚠3 N 47°46.499' W 121°51.031'

⚠4 N 47°46.882' W 121°52.770'

⚠5 N 47°44.872' W 121°53.379'

To Hwy 203, Duvall

To Sultan

N

Marckworth State Forest

Creek

Cherry

260'

1,070'

590' ℗

END
BEGIN

To Duvall

0   1/2   1
MILE

Prelude

Denoting the first rise of the Cascade foothills, the Marckworth Forest straddles the border of King and Snohomish Counties just east of State Route 203 between Monroe and Duvall. The Marckworth, known more for its luxuriant growth than its choppy topography, percolates water from marshy lowland to marshy lowland, gradually channeling water to the south, west, and north; Stossel Creek, Cherry Creek, and Youngs Creek feed the Tolt, Snoqualmie, and Skykomish Rivers, respectively. Unfortunately, the Washington State Department of Natural Resources manages this gigantic parcel of land for timber, clearcutting "units" and building roads with little regard for the area's delicate hydrology. Additionally, the DNR allocates zero resources to any recreation opportunity in the Marckworth, so information is scarce and maps nonexistent. They could do a much better job at working with trails groups to expand recreational opportunities, limit recreational shooting, and clean up this beautiful but beleaguered forest. Mountain bikers should lobby state and county governments to designate the Marckworth a gigantic regional park. It's simply too beautiful, too big, and too close to the populations of Everett and Seattle to continue the current timber harvesting practices or allow the land to be developed. For the time being, though, remember that logging trucks and some utility vehicles may be on even the gated dirt roads. Also, be aware that biosolids get sprayed in the Marckworth, and certain stretches of road don't always have that sweet Christmas-tree smell.

To Get There

From Seattle, take State Route 520 east to Redmond, then continue straight on Avondale Road. Turn right on Woodinville-Duvall Road toward Duvall. After crossing the Snoqualmie River, turn left on SR 203 in Duvall. After one block, bear right on Northeast Cherry Valley Road and start your odometer. At 4.4 miles, bear right on Kelly Road Northeast. At 6.9 miles, take a hard left onto Northeast Stossel Creek Way. At 8.4 miles, bear right onto Stossel Creek Road Northeast, which is dirt, and enter the Marckworth Forest. At 9.6 miles, reach a four-way intersection and park (the roads to the right and left are gated, but don't block them).

The Ride

From the four-way intersection, pedal along Stossel Creek Road, paralleling Stossel Creek, which is below on the right. At **1.2** miles, turn left onto gated road CV-100 and begin climbing. (Note: If you want to avoid the four-mile ridge-top excursion that follows, continue up Stossel Creek Road for about one and three-quarter miles and rejoin the route at the 5.3-mile mark. This shaves about two and one-half miles from the loop.) During the climb, ignore a lesser road on the left at **1.7** miles and two

A wet section of trail in the Marckworth Forest

bermed roads on the right at **2.1** miles. Crest the top of the hill at **2.3** miles, then descend to a four-way intersection at **2.4** miles. Turn right onto ST-2000. Stay on the main road to a fork, **2.8** miles, and bear left on ST-2100.

Descend quickly to a fork at **3.1** miles. Bear right onto CV-105 and enter a deep, second-growth forest, and continue descending. Pass CV-105B on the right at **3.3** miles, and continue to descend on CV-105 to a gravel pit at **4.2** miles. Make a hairpin turn to the right and immediately begin climbing the rough road out from the gravel pit. The ascent eases at **4.4** miles, then levels in a short distance. Ignore a road on the left at **4.6** miles. Just around the corner, reach ST-2000, turn left, and descend. At **5.3** miles reach a gate where the northern end of ST-2000 meets Stossel Creek Road: Turn left and ride north on this main Marckworth artery. Pedal up this road—passing a road on the left and then crossing Cherry Creek—to a fork at **6.2** miles: Turn left.

From the fork, gradually descend on this well-used dirt road. Stay on the main road. At a fork, **7.6** miles, bear left, riding southwest now, and begin a gradual climb through, alternately, second-growth and clearcuts.

Stay on the main road to a fork at **9.5** miles and take a hard left turn onto a less maintained road. This unmarked road heads south, dropping quickly toward Cherry Creek. After several quick switchbacks, the way levels somewhat at around the **11**-mile mark. When the road forks at **11.4** miles, bear left. The road ends at **11.9** miles, but take the well-used trail that starts up from the terminus and continues south. At **12.1** miles the trail reaches a road: Angle left, riding along this uneven road, which parallels Cherry Creek. At **13** miles, the rough road ends at a dirt road. Turn left and descend to a bridge over the creek. **WHOA!** Cross with extreme care.

From the eastern bank of Cherry Creek, the dirt road cuts steeply upward. The road becomes a doubletrack, then levels at **13.4** miles. Pass a small pretzel of trails on the right, then descend on the doubletrack to a washout at **13.8**. From the washout, the doubletrack climbs a short distance, then bends right, becoming a trail (or a large puddle, depending on the time of year). At **14** miles, the trail ends at a road, CV-115: Turn left. Reach a fork at **14.3** miles and go right. Continue the climb away from Cherry Creek. At **14.6** miles, arrive at a fork and bear left (the right fork skirts the bank of a small lake). At **14.9** miles, take the right fork, then at **15.5** miles bear to the left, ignoring a spur on the right. Still climbing, reach another fork at **16.1** miles and bear right. At **16.5** miles, reach the four-way intersection: Turn right on ST-2000 and continue the ascent, angling south up a broad ridge. A mile farther, the ascent eases somewhat as the road meanders across the top of the ridge, affording views of the Cascade range to the left. Crest the ride's high point at **18.1** miles. From here, the road careens down to a gate at the junction of ST-2000 and Stossel Creek Road to complete the loop, **19** miles.

Gazetteer

Nearby camping: Tolt-John MacDonald Park (King County Parks), Tinkham Campground (USFS)
Nearest food, drink, services: Duvall

SNOQUALMIE RIVER
9 Tolt Pipeline Trail
✪

Distance	9.2 miles
Ride	Out & Back; gated dirt road
Duration	1 to 2 hours
Travel time	Seattle—1 hour; Bellingham—2 hours
Hill factor	Rolling hills; 460-foot gain
Skill level	Beginner
Season	Year-round
Maps	USGS: Carnation
Users	Bicyclists, equestrians, hikers
More info	King County Parks, 206-296-4232

Prelude

With much the same character as its western sibling (which runs between Woodinville and the Snoqualmie River), this section of the Tolt Pipeline Trail is an easy ride on a wide, gravelly, nonmotorized utility road. Over rolling topography, the trail parallels the Tolt Pipeline, one of Seattle's main water arteries. Pedal past semirural, semisuburban homes, as well as larger tracts of undeveloped land. Watch for equestrians and pedestrians—primarily dog walkers—along the route. From the end of the route described below, the trail continues east to the Tolt Reservoir; however, there's no reason to ride that stretch because the trail becomes uncomfortably rough and follows a paved road, compromising the scenery. The winter day I scouted this trail, I could look west and see scattered sun shining on the Olympic Mountains, though when I looked down the trail to the east, dark clouds huddled at the foothills of the Cascades. As I reached the turnaround point, light snow fell as a winter storm brewed.

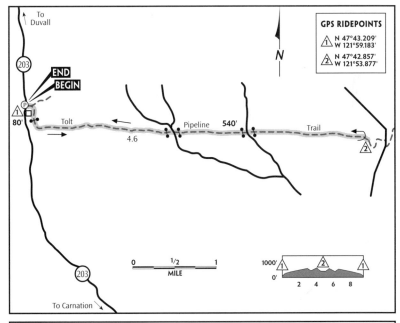

To Get There

From Seattle, take State Route 520 east to Redmond, then continue straight on Avondale Road. Turn right on Woodinville-Duvall Road toward Duvall. After crossing the Snoqualmie River, turn right on SR 203 in Duvall. From Duvall, drive south on SR 203. At about 1.5 miles, turn right into the parking area for Duvall Park.

The Ride

From the paved parking area at Duvall Park, carefully cross SR 203 to the dirt road opposite. The dirt road immediately divides: Take the right fork, passing through a gate and gradually climbing past the water maintenance building on the right. The dirt road meets the gravelly pipeline road at **0.3** mile. Bear left and pedal up the wide road. At **0.5** mile, ride around the first of numerous gates that keep motorized vehicles off the pipeline maintenance road. The sign reads "Pipeline Right of Way." The road rises and falls, though it gradually gains elevation. At **2** miles, ride around several gates, then cross paved Big Rock Road. Reach the ride's high point at **3** miles. Descend for a short distance and cross O'Dell Road at **3.2** miles. At an overlook, **4.6** miles, the maintenance road veers sharply to the right and switchbacks down. Turn around here, retracing your pedal strokes back to SR 203 to complete the ride, **9.2** miles.

Gazetteer

Nearby camping: Tolt-John MacDonald Park (King County Parks), Tinkham Campground (USFS)
Nearest food, drink, services: Duvall

10 | Snoqualmie Valley Trail

⚙⚙

Distance	20.2 miles
Ride	Out & Back; dirt and gravel rail-trail
Duration	2 to 4 hours
Travel time	Seattle—45 minutes; Ellensburg—2 hours
Hill factor	Nearly flat, very easy grade; 410-foot gain
Skill level	Beginner
Season	Year-round
Maps	USGS: Carnation, Fall City, Snoqualmie
Users	Bicyclists, equestrians, hikers
More info	King County Parks, 206-296-4232

Prelude

I've ridden the Snoqualmie Valley Trail many, many times, most recently on a soggy, early June day. I didn't get too wet, though, because the trail is compact and not prone to puddling, and the light tree canopy pro-

Crossing the Tolt River on the Snoqualmie Valley Trail

tected us from some of the weather. Easy, nontechnical trails like this are sometimes just what the doctor ordered. This section of the old Milwaukee Railroad grade, converted now to a rail-trail, stretches from Carnation to Snoqualmie. It's perfect for families because the wide trail allows cyclists to ride side by side and converse, and the gentle grade won't leave anyone behind.

To Get There

From Interstate 90 at Preston, about 22 miles east of Seattle, take the Preston–Fall City Road to Fall City. Start your odometer from the junction of State Route 202 and SR 203 in Fall City, and proceed north on SR 203. Drive about 5.5 miles to Carnation, then turn right (east) onto Entwhistle Street. At 5.8 miles, park at Nick Loutsis Park on the right.

The Ride

The Snoqualmie Valley Trail passes adjacent to Nick Loutsis Park. Facing the wide, gravelly rail-trail from the parking area, turn right and pedal south. You will soon appreciate the topographic mastery of those early railroad engineers, as the trail ascends at an almost imperceptible rate. At **0.5** mile, the trail crosses the Tolt River. Pass Remlinger Farms on the left, **0.6** mile. The way winds easily upward. Ride around several gates and cross a number of roads along the way. At **6.5** miles, pedal across a new bridge. At **8.6** miles, Mount Si looms ahead as the trail bends around to the left. At **9.1** miles, cross a high bridge above Tokul Creek. This is a wonderful place to stop for a moment and take in the views of the valley and the creek far below. At **10.1** miles, reach a short tunnel under Tokul Road. Turn around here and ride back to Nick Loutsis Park to complete the route, **20.2** miles.

Option

From the tunnel, it's a short trip to Snoqualmie Falls. Ride about 100 yards farther up the rail-trail, and take a narrow trail on the left that leads to a paved road. Turn left on the road and ride to the intersection of Tokul Road and Southeast 60th Street, 10.6 miles. From here, turn left and ride down Tokul Road to SR 202, turn right, and almost immediately find the parking area for Snoqualmie Falls on the left, 1.3 miles from the tunnel under Tokul Road. This option adds 2.6 miles to the ride.

Gazetteer

Nearby camping: Tolt-John MacDonald Park (King County Parks), Tinkham Campground (USFS)

Nearest food, drink, services: Carnation, Fall City

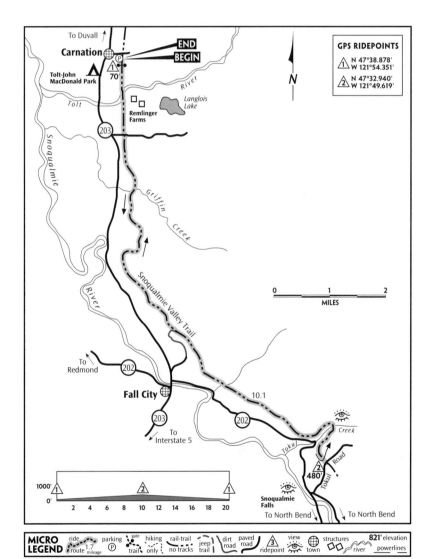

11 SNOQUALMIE RIVER
CCC Road
☺☺☺

Distance	20 miles
Ride	Out & Back; doubletrack, dirt road
Duration	3 to 5 hours
Travel time	Seattle—1 hour; Ellensburg—1.5 hours
Hill factor	Strenuous first mile, some bushwhacking; 760-foot gain
Skill level	Advanced
Season	Spring, summer, fall
Maps	Green Trails: Bandera, Mount Si; USFS: North Bend Ranger District
Users	Bicyclists, equestrians, hikers
More info	Mount Baker-Snoqualmie National Forest, North Bend District, 425-888-1421

Prelude

The Forest Service has plans to improve the CCC Road by constructing a new trail that will originate from the Mount Si trailhead, connect to the existing CCC Road, and then extend east to the Taylor River Road via a singletrack. That would certainly be a nice long trail and a good mountain-bike opportunity. But with their recent closure of the nearby Middle Fork Trail—the only *true* trail open to mountain bikes in their entire district—cycling opportunities planned by the North Bend Ranger District should be regarded as suspect. In the meantime (and that could

Cruising the CCC Road

be forever), the CCC Road, which is gated at either end, provides a rough, adventurous trip high up the northern slope of the Middle Fork of the Snoqualmie River. Several washouts and some overly ambitious alder growth force a couple of short walks, but certainly keep it interesting.

To Get There

Take Interstate 90 to exit 31 at North Bend. Turn left at the end of the interstate ramp onto North Bend Boulevard. Turn right onto East North Bend Way. Drive through town, then take a left onto Southeast Mount Si Road, and zero out your odometer. At 2.5 miles, after many bends and twists in the road, pass Mount Si trailhead on the left. At 3.7 miles, find an unmarked, gated road on the left, and park.

The Ride

Do not ride up the gated dirt road. Instead, pedal up the paved road, away from Mount Si trailhead. Immediately steep, the road turns to gravel after one-quarter mile, and continues climbing through an older

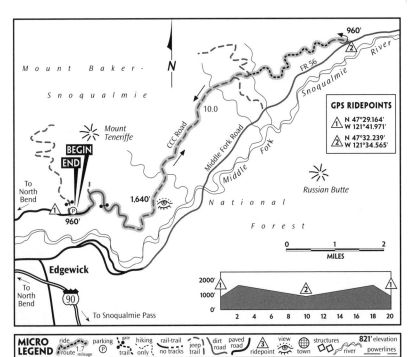

clearcut. Ignore several lesser spurs off the main road, then at **1.1** miles pass around a yellow gate and continue up. When the way forks at **1.5** miles, take the left fork. Reach a four-way intersection at the top of the hill, the ride's high point, at **2.1** miles. The crest of the hill and a recent clearcut afford expansive views of Mount Garfield and the entire Middle Fork of the Snoqualmie River valley. Travel straight through the four-way intersection, continuing on the main road. Swing around the southern edge of a small plateau, and gradually descend. At **3** miles, the road forks at a large rock—go left. Take a second left when the road forks again at **3.2** miles. The plateau gives way to a steep hillside just before a stream crossing, and the road, now a jeep track, traverses the steep slope into a heavier forest, **4.4** miles.

One mile farther, ride back into an older clearcut. The gradual downhill traverse is sometimes a rocky creek bed, other times a smooth, forested jeep trail. The trail crosses numerous creeks, some intermittent, some perennial Middle Fork tributaries. At **6.8** miles, cross a substantial creek. Just beyond, the jeep track hits a T at a more-traveled dirt road: Bear left and ride into a nicely forested area. (The right fork drops down to the Middle Fork Road in slightly more than one mile.)

At **7.2** miles, as the main road bends to the left, take a lesser fork on the right. **WHOA!** This grassy old jeep trail is easy to miss. Here's where this ride really gets interesting. Since the jeep trail hasn't been used much, young alder and Douglas fir saplings have grown up from the trail's tread; shrubs and vines have filled in the flanks. Though mostly ridable (with eye protection), this section is in serious need of brushing and may require some hike-a-biking after vital growth spurts. At **8.8** miles, find an enormous tree across the trail. Find a walkaround on the left. From the blowdown, continue pedaling downward on the rutted jeep trail. At **9.5** miles reach a huge washout that has obliterated the route. Walk over the boulders to the trail on the opposite side. At **9.6** miles, the jeep trail forks—turn downhill to the right. After a short, but steep and rocky, descent, arrive at Middle Fork Road, **10** miles. From here, turn around and retrace your tracks to the start to complete the Out & Back, **20** miles.

Gazetteer

Nearby camping: Tinkham Campground (USFS), Tolt-John MacDonald Park (King County Parks)
Nearest food, drink, services: North Bend

12 WENATCHEE
Little Camas Creek Epic

⊕⊕⊕⊕⊕

Distance	31.3 miles
Ride	Loop; singletrack, dirt road; views
Duration	5 to 8 hours
Travel time	Wenatchee—30 minutes; Seattle—3 hours
Hill factor	Grueling trail climbs, hike-a-bikes; 3,480-foot gain
Skill level	Advanced
Season	Summer, fall
Maps	Green Trails: Liberty; USFS: Leavenworth Ranger District
Users	Bicyclists, equestrians, hikers, motorcyclists
More info	Wenatchee National Forest, Leavenworth District, 509-548-6977

Steep switchbacks near Little Camas Creek

Prelude

Long, arduous climbs, numerous hike-a-bikes, and some difficult route-finding qualify this as an epic. I thought I was lost a number of times over the course of this ride, as I navigated the brushy, unmarked trails and ancient, no-longer-mapped roads that form this loop. But flush with successful exploration, elated at huge elevation gain conquered, and left with two hours of daylight to spare (hard to believe), I turned from Tronsen Ridge Trail onto Red Hill Trail and began one of the smoothest, sweetest singletrack descents around. I could enjoy the corkscrewing drop largely because of multiple energy bars, several racks of Fig Newtons, and lots of water—the high, open hillsides along Tronsen Ridge can be scorching in August. When crossing Red Hill, be sure to stop and check out the weird rock formations and sheer cliffs that hang above Devils Gulch.

To Get There

Take US Highway 2 over Stevens Pass to Leavenworth. Continue east on US 2 to the town of Cashmere. From US 2 at Cashmere, turn right onto Division Street and zero your odometer. At 0.6 mile, Division becomes Pioneer Avenue. At 0.7 mile, turn left onto Mission Creek Road. When the pavement ends at a fork, 7.8 miles, turn left onto Forest Road 7100. At 10.4 miles, find Devils Gulch trailhead on the right, and park.

The Ride

From Devils Gulch trailhead, ride back toward Cashmere on FR 7100. Stay on the main road, descending, to a fork at **2.6** miles. Turn left onto FR 7104 and begin a gradual ascent. At **2.8** miles, bear right, away from the private driveway. When the dirt road divides at **3.7** miles, take the left fork, which is gated. Continue the gradual climb up FR 7104. At **3.9** miles, pass by Red Hill Trail 1223. The road narrows slightly, but the tread is solid and the grade moderate. Just as the road elbows to the left and begins a steep climb, **5.3** miles, bear right onto a rugged old road. WHOA! This is not an intuitive turn. The old road peters out at **5.5** miles and an unmarked singletrack continues up the narrow Little Camas Creek valley.

The lightly used singletrack creeps up the valley at a moderate rate; however, after the **6.1**-mile point the grade becomes quite steep. Switchbacking up the steep, forested valley, the trail cuts northwest, away from

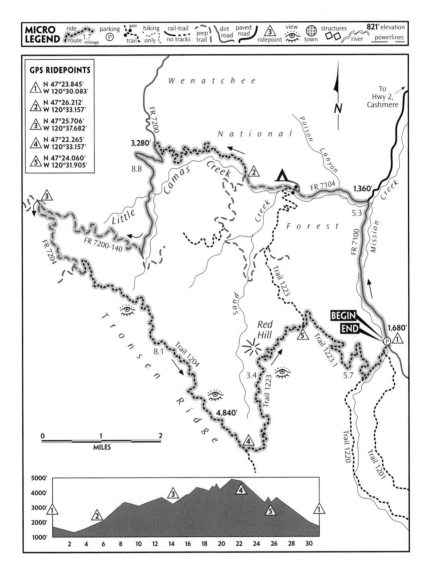

the canyon-hidden creek, and much of the next two miles is a hike-a-bike. At **8.3** miles, reach FR 7200, turn left, and continue the ascent. The dirt road winds upward to a high point, **8.6** miles, offering views to the east. From here, the road descends into the Little Camas Creek valley, which is wide at this point. After crossing a bridge over the creek at **10.1** miles, stay on the main road as you begin a gradual climb across the meadow. The road forks at **11.1** miles: Take a hard right turn onto FR 7200-140, which is narrow and, in places, rutted. Continue the gradual climb through a thin forest, mounting the north end of Tronsen Ridge.

At **12.7** miles, reach a saddle that affords excellent views of the Stuart Range ahead to the northwest. Leaving the saddle, zip down the narrow, winding road. At **14.1** miles, reach a fork and turn left on FR 7204. Don't hold back on your consumption of sweet-rich-doughy things, because the next seven miles will suck out your very last Thanksgiving Day calorie and spit you out like a discarded peel. The road, rough and narrow, climbs steadily, heading south up Tronsen Ridge. Ignore a gated road on the right at **15.8** miles. But just around the corner, **16** miles, turn left at the fork and ride over a berm. The road soon narrows to singletrack and climbs at a hectic rate through a scattered pine forest. The trail, faint now and overgrown in sections, forks at a saddle, **17** miles: Bear left and begin descending. **WHOA!** The next mile is somewhat confusing, so try to stay on the main trail, ignoring several lesser trails on the right and left.

At **18** miles, reach a fork and bear left on Tronsen Ridge Trail 1204. At **18.1** miles, reach a T and turn right. From here, the trail is quite over-grown; pushing through thick, abrasive shrubs is your likely fortune. The way opens up and descends for a short distance, but then climbs straight up, necessitating a push, to the **18.9**-mile point. Ride along the jagged ridge top, which constantly drops and climbs, drops and climbs. Follow a ragged dirt road past an obscure campsite; then, at **19.6** miles, bear left on Tronsen Ridge Trail 1204 and begin yet another climb. The trail, which switchbacks up the sparsely forested ridge, is smooth, distinct, and quite ridable—if you're still fresh.

Crest the ride's high point at **21.1** miles, then traverse downward. After another climb, reach a fork at **22.2** miles and bear left on Red Hill Trail 1223. No matter how wasted you feel, the next nine miles will have you smiling again. Watch out for other trail users! After a series of fast, roaring switchbacks, cross Red Hill, and traverse past a number of huge rocks that form the crooked spine of the ridge between Sand Creek and Devils Gulch. The ridge top beyond Red Hill rolls and swells, occasionally requiring a short push. At **25.6** miles, reach a fork and bear right on Red Hill Spur Trail 1223.1 toward Devils Gulch. One more strenuous climb to go: Hike-a-bike to the **26.6**-mile point. From here, the stable, well-main-tained trail switchbacks and corkscrews down into Devils Gulch, making the next three miles one of the best singletrack descents around. Again,

The Stuart Range from Tronsen Ridge

watch out for other trail users. Reach a T at **30.2** miles and turn left on Devils Gulch Trail 1220. The trail parallels Mission Creek. Pass Mission Ridge Trail on the right at **31.1** miles, then pass Red Devil Trail on the right at **31.2** miles. At **31.3** miles, reach Devils Gulch trailhead to complete the loop, wayworn but ready for a trip to Rusty's in Cashmere.

Gazetteer

Nearby camping: Sites at end of FR 7104 (USFS, primitive), Eightmile Campground (USFS)
Nearest food, drink, services: Cashmere

13 Red Hill

☺☺☺

Distance	17.3 miles
Ride	Loop; singletrack, dirt road
Duration	3 to 5 hours
Travel time	Wenatchee—30 minutes; Seattle—3 hours
Hill factor	Tough dirt-road climb, some short walks; 2,280-foot gain
Skill level	Intermediate
Season	Summer, fall
Maps	Green Trails: Liberty; USFS: Leavenworth Ranger District
Users	Bicyclists, equestrians, hikers, motorcyclists
More info	Wenatchee National Forest, Leavenworth District, 509-548-6977

Prelude

An October rain fell while I tried to sort out all the dirt roads and double-tracks and spurs and unmarked trails that crisscross the steep slope between Little Camas Creek and Sand Creek. Damp, clay-rich soil impeded my progress. My map got wet. But the mucky soils and wayward roads were forgotten after I reached Red Hill Trail, one of the nicest singletrack descents around. This is like the younger brother to the Little Camas Creek Epic (Ride 12).

To Get There

Take US Highway 2 over Stevens Pass to Leavenworth. Continue east on US 2 to the town of Cashmere. From US 2 at Cashmere, turn right onto Division Street and zero your odometer. At 0.6 mile, Division becomes Pioneer Avenue. At 0.7 mile, turn left onto Mission Creek Road. When the pavement ends at a fork, 7.8 miles, turn left onto Forest Road 7100. At 10.4 miles, find Devils Gulch trailhead on the right, and park.

The Ride

From Devils Gulch trailhead, ride back toward Cashmere on FR 7100. Stay on the main road. Descend to a fork at **2.6** miles, and turn left onto FR 7104. At **2.8** miles, bear right, away from the private driveway. When the dirt road divides at **3.7** miles, take the left fork, which is gated. Continue the gradual climb up FR 7104. At **3.9** miles, pass by Red Hill Trail 1223. Ignore a lesser dirt road on the right at **5.3** miles. The road hairpins left here, and begins a steep climb. Reach a fork at **6.4** miles and bear left, remaining on the main road. The road becomes a double-track, carving a rolling traverse on the slopes above Sand Creek. At **7.4** miles, reach a fork and bear left, descending quickly.

When you reach a fork at **9.3** miles, bear left and begin a steep climb up a rocky road. At a sharp right-hand bend in the road, **9.8** miles, find an unmarked trail on the right. Take this trail. For the first quarter mile, the clay-rich soil may make the moderate climb unridable,

Toward Red Hill on Trail 1223

especially on wet days. But soon the solid, pine-needled tread allows for good traction as the trail climbs south. At **11.6** miles, reach a T and turn left on Red Hill Spur Trail 1223.1 toward Devils Gulch. For the next mile, the trail is steep and may be a hike-a-bike to the top at **12.6** miles.

From here, the stable, well-maintained trail switchbacks and corkscrews down into Devils Gulch, making the next three miles one of the best singletrack descents around. Don't spook other trail users with out-of-control riding. Reach a T at **16.2** miles and turn left on Devils Gulch Trail 1220. The trail traverses the open slopes just above Mission

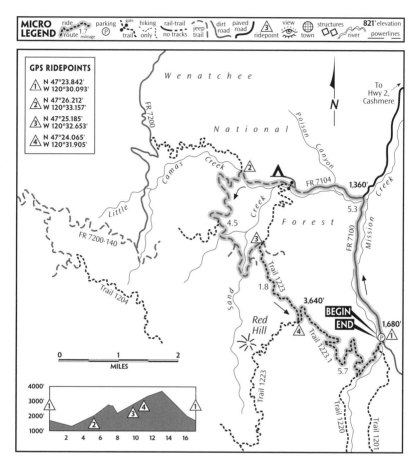

Creek. Pass Mission Ridge Trail on the right at **17.1** miles, then pass Red Devil Trail on the left at **17.2** miles. At **17.3** miles, reach the Devils Gulch trailhead to complete the loop.

Gazetteer

Nearby camping: Sites at end of FR 7104 (USFS, primitive), Eightmile Campground (USFS)

Nearest food, drink, services: Cashmere

14 Devils Gulch

WENATCHEE

✦✦✦✦

Distance	24.9 miles
Ride	Loop; singletrack, dirt road
Duration	4 to 6 hours
Travel time	Wenatchee—30 minutes; Seattle—3 hours
Hill factor	Long, relentless dirt-road climb; 3,380-foot gain
Skill level	Intermediate
Season	Summer, fall
Maps	USFS: Leavenworth Ranger District
Users	Bicyclists, equestrians, hikers, motorcyclists
More info	Wenatchee National Forest, Leavenworth District, 509-548-6977

Another fast ride through Devils Gulch

Prelude

Known as one of Washington State's classic rides, Devils Gulch lives up to the hype in many respects. Some cyclists, loathe to pedal the eleven-mile, 3,300-foot climb that starts this loop, shuttle a car to the trailhead and begin riding from the top. To give you an idea of how continuous and unabated the descent is, I once saw a rider complete a one-way trip from the top on a one-speed BMX-style bike. Rumors have it that sections of this trail fall inside a timber unit scheduled for cutting. Call ahead to check on the status of the trail. Also, strong riders have been known to ride up Devils Gulch Trail, walk up the switchbacks, and then ride down Mission Ridge Trail. Don't run them (or any other trail user) down during this fast, winding descent.

To Get There

Take US Highway 2 over Stevens Pass to Leavenworth. Continue east on US 2 to the town of Cashmere. From US 2 at Cashmere, turn right onto Division Street and zero your odometer. At 0.6 mile, Division becomes Pioneer Avenue. At 0.7 mile, turn left onto Mission Creek Road. When the pavement ends at a fork, 7.8 miles, turn left onto Forest Road 7100. At 10.4 miles, find Devils Gulch trailhead on the right, and park.

The Ride

From the trailhead, ride up FR 7100, heading south. The road ascends at an easy rate to a fork at **2.6** miles. Bear to the right, remaining on FR 7100, and continue the climb, which soon becomes more rigorous (Twinkies, doughnuts, and candy bars are good things). Stay on the main road, ignoring several lesser spurs. At **7.6** miles, round a hairpin turn, passing a spur on the right. The wide turn provides a fine view of Mission Ridge, Tronsen Ridge, and the Wenatchee Mountains. At **9.3** miles, cross a cattle grate and reach a four-way intersection: Take a hard right, continuing on FR 7100. Pass through a gate, then reach a T at **10** miles and turn right onto FR 9712 (Liberty-Beehive Road). Ignore a spur road on the right at **10.5** miles. At **11.9** miles, find the Devils Gulch Trail 1220 trailhead on the right.

The trail begins from the end of the parking area, heading downhill to the northwest. After a fast, traversing descent, reach a four-way intersection at **15.2** miles: Go straight, continuing down Devils Gulch Trail 1220. A few turns down the trail, begin descending a hectic set of switchbacks

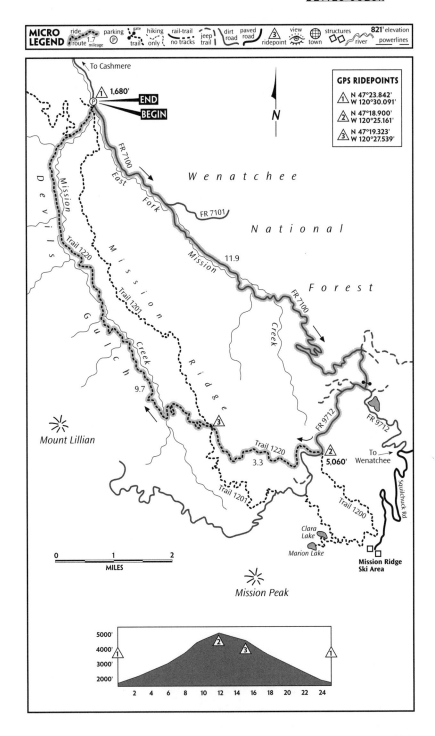

MICRO LEGEND — ride route · 1.7 mileage · parking (P) · gate trail · hiking only trail · rail-trail no tracks · jeep trail · dirt road · paved road · 3 ridepoint · view town · structures · river · 821' elevation · powerlines

To Cashmere

1 1,680'

END
BEGIN

N

GPS RIDEPOINTS

1 N 47°23.842'
   W 120°30.091'

2 N 47°18.900'
   W 120°25.161'

3 N 47°19.323'
   W 120°27.539'

W e n a t c h e e

FR 7100

East Fork

FR 7101

N a t i o n a l

Mission

11.9

Devils

Mission

Trail 1220

Trail 1201

M i s s i o n

R i d g e

F o r e s t

FR 7100

Creek

G u l c h

Creek

9.7

FR 9712

FR 9712

Mount Lillian

3

Trail 1220

3.3

2 5,060'

To Wenatchee

Squilchuck Rd

Trail 1201

Trail 1200

Clara Lake

Marion Lake

Mission Ridge Ski Area

Mission Peak

0   1   2
MILES

5000'
4000'
3000'
2000'

1   2   3   1

2   4   6   8   10   12   14   16   18   20   22   24

into Devils Gulch. At **17.5** miles, reach Mission Creek. The grade eases here as the trail bends north and descends through the healthy forest. The trail, for the most part well maintained, crosses Mission Creek several times. At **23.9** miles, bypass Red Hill Trail on the left. At **24.8** miles, ignore Mission Ridge Trail on the right. At **24.8** miles, bypass Red Devil Trail on the left. Just around the corner, **24.9** miles, reach Devils Gulch trailhead to complete the loop.

Gazetteer

Nearby camping: Sites at end of FR 7104 (USFS, primitive), Eightmile Campground (USFS)
Nearest food, drink, services: Cashmere

15

WENATCHEE
Mission Ridge
✿✿✿✿

Distance	26.3 miles
Ride	Loop; singletrack, dirt road; views
Duration	4 to 7 hours
Travel time	Wenatchee—30 minutes; Seattle—3 hours
Hill factor	Long, relentless dirt-road climb; 4,020-foot gain
Skill level	Advanced
Season	Summer, fall
Maps	USFS: Leavenworth Ranger District
Users	Bicyclists, equestrians, hikers, motorcyclists
More info	Wenatchee National Forest, Leavenworth District, 509-548-6977

Rocky crest of Mission Ridge

Prelude

Mission Ridge is the lesser-known, fraternal twin of Devils Gulch (Ride 14). Both rides begin with the same eleven-mile dirt-road climb, but when the Devils Gulch Trail bails out, the Mission Ridge Loop continues ascending more than 600 feet farther. Of course, to use an old adage, what goes up must come down, so you can think of it as just that much more descending to come. Though Mission Ridge is rocky in places and generally more challenging than its gulch twin, its high ridge, cliffs, and massive basalt formations make this a more exhilarating ride. In fact, after one friend rode this Mission Ridge route, he said, "I'll never ride Devils Gulch again."

To Get There

Take US Highway 2 over Stevens Pass to Leavenworth. Continue east on US 2 to the town of Cashmere. From US 2 at Cashmere, turn right onto Division Street and zero your odometer. At 0.6 mile, Division becomes Pioneer Avenue. At 0.7 mile, turn left onto Mission Creek Road. When the pavement ends at a fork, 7.8 miles, turn left onto Forest Road 7100. At 10.4 miles, find Devils Gulch trailhead on the right, and park.

The Ride

From the trailhead, ride up FR 7100, heading south. The road ascends at an easy rate to a fork at **2.6** miles. Bear to the right, remaining on FR 7100, and continue the climb, which becomes more rigorous. Stay on the main road, ignoring several lesser spurs, as you climb through a thin pine forest. At **7.6** miles, round a hairpin turn, passing a spur on the right. The wide turn provides a fine view of Mission Ridge, Tronsen Ridge, and the Wenatchee Mountains (time to break out that rack of Fig Newtons you have stowed in your fanny pack). At **9.3** miles, cross a cattle grate and reach a four-way intersection: Take a hard right, continuing on FR 7100. Pass through a gate, then reach a T at **10** miles and turn right onto FR 9712 (Liberty-Beehive Road). Ignore a spur road on the right at **10.5** miles. At **11.9** miles, pass Devils Gulch trailhead on the right. Continue up FR 9712.

At **13.1** miles, pass Pipeline Trail on the left. At **13.7** miles, reach the Mission Ridge Trail 1201 trailhead on the right. Ride out Trail 1201, at times rocky and technical, and drop headlong down Mission Ridge. At **17.7** miles, reach a four-way intersection with Devils Gulch Trail:

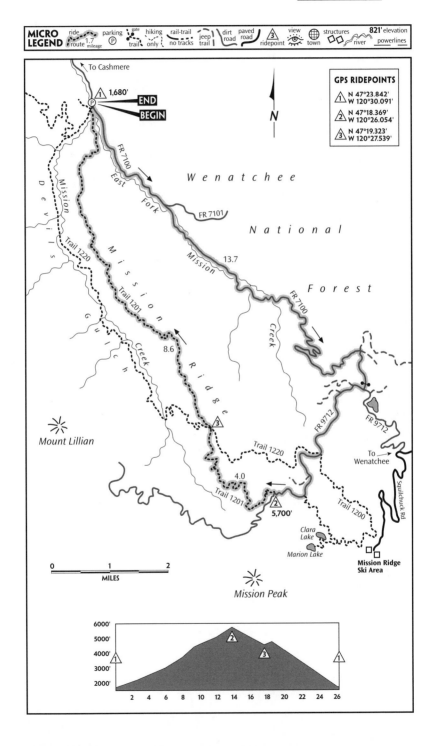

Basalt fields on Trail 1201

Continue straight on Mission Ridge Trail 1201. From here, the trail climbs steeply up the ridge's spine, requiring a hike-a-bike. Top out at **18.5** miles, and begin the backbone descent. Traverse across several steep, rocky slopes. At **22.4** miles, start the sustained drop toward Devils Gulch, cruising through an open pine forest. At **26.1** miles, cross a short bridge over Mission Creek to a T, and turn right on Devils Gulch Trail 1220. Pass Red Devil Trail on the left at **26.2** miles. Reach Devils Gulch trailhead at **26.3** miles to complete the loop.

Gazetteer

Nearby camping: Sites at end of FR 7104 (USFS, primitive), Eightmile Campground (USFS)

Nearest food, drink, services: Cashmere

16

WENATCHEE
Pipeline Trail
✹✹✹

Distance	12.2 miles
Ride	Loop; singletrack, dirt road
Duration	2 to 3 hours
Travel time	Wenatchee—30 minutes; Seattle—3 hours
Hill factor	Steep climbs, hike-a-bike; 1,180-foot gain
Skill level	Advanced
Season	Summer, fall
Maps	USFS: Leavenworth Ranger District
Users	Bicyclists, equestrians, hikers, motorcyclists
More info	Wenatchee National Forest, Leavenworth District, 509-548-6977

Prelude

For those who aren't interested in giant elevation gains but don't mind a few technical switchbacks, this more modest route could be for you. Traversing the slopes between Mission Ridge Ski Area and the head of Devils Gulch is fast and fun, with two scenic lakes and a few rocky challenges thrown in for good measure. But plan on a few stretches of hike-a-biking. Hard-core riders may want to incorporate this ride into a Devils Gulch (Ride 14) or Mission Ridge (Ride 15) day.

To Get There

Take US Highway 2 over Stevens Pass to Leavenworth. Continue east on US 2 to the town of Cashmere. From US 2 at Cashmere, turn right onto Division Street and zero your odometer. At 0.6 mile, Division becomes Pioneer Avenue. At 0.7 mile, turn left onto Mission Creek Road. When the pavement ends at a fork, 7.8 miles, turn left onto Forest Road 7100. At 10.4 miles, pass Devils Gulch trailhead on the right. At a fork, 13 miles, bear to the right, continuing up FR 7100. Stay on the main road, ignoring lesser spurs. At 19.7 miles, reach a four-way intersection: Turn right, continuing up FR 7100. Reach a T at 20.4 miles and turn right onto FR 9712 (Liberty-Beehive Road). At 22.3 miles, find Devils Gulch trailhead on the right. Park here. (Alternate route: From Wenatchee, take Squilchuck Road (County Road 711) toward Mission Ridge Ski Area. Turn right on FR 9712 (Liberty-Beehive Road) toward Beehive Reservoir. After about 4 miles, find Devils Gulch trailhead on the right.)

The Ride

Across FR 9712 from Devils Gulch trailhead, find Pipeline Trail 1200 and take it. The trail traverses south toward Mission Ridge Ski Area. At **2.3** miles, ignore a trail down to Mission Ridge Ski Area on the left. Almost immediately, turn right and grunt up a series of loose, steep switchbacks toward Clara and Marion Lakes. At **3.2** miles, reach a T: Go right, following the signs toward Liberty-Beehive Road (the lakes can be found less than one-quarter mile off to the left). The next section of trail is quite rocky and requires advanced bike-handling skills. At **3.9** miles, crest the top, then descend to Liberty-Beehive Road (aka FR 9712) at **4.3** miles. Turn left on the dirt road and climb at a moderate rate. At **4.9** miles, find the Mission Ridge Trail 1201 trailhead on the right. Take this trail.

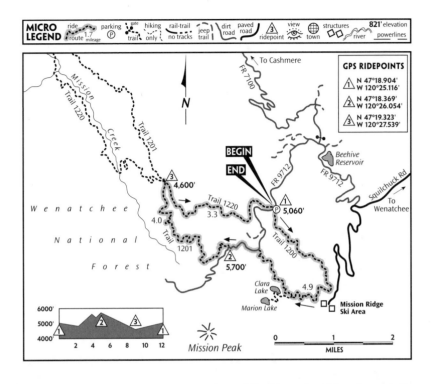

MICRO LEGEND ride route 1.7 mileage | parking (P) | gate | hiking trail | only | rail-trail no tracks | jeep trail | dirt road | paved road | 3 ridepoint | view | town | structures | 821' elevation | river | powerlines

To Cashmere

FR 7100

N

BEGIN
END

GPS RIDEPOINTS
1 N 47°18.904'
W 120°25.116'
2 N 47°18.369'
W 120°26.054'
3 N 47°19.323'
W 120°27.539'

Mission Trail 1220

Creek

Trail 1201

FR 9712

Beehive Reservoir

FR 9712

Squilchuck Rd.

3 4,600'

Trail 1220
3.3

1 P 5,060'

To Wenatchee

W e n a t c h e e

4.0

Trail 1201

Trail 1200

N a t i o n a l

2 5,700'

F o r e s t

Clara Lake

4.9

Mission Ridge Ski Area

Marion Lake

6000'
5000'
4000'
2 4 6 8 10 12

1 2 3 1

Mission Peak

0 1 2
MILES

From the trailhead, the trail heads rapidly down the ridge through fir and pine; the trail is still somewhat technical, but less so than Pipeline Trail. At **8.9** miles, reach a four-way intersection: Turn right onto Devils Gulch Trail 1220. This trail, the mama bear trail, is smoothest of all, and it ascends through big trees on an even tread. Arrive back at Devils Gulch trailhead at **12.2** miles to complete the loop.

Gazetteer

Nearby camping: Sites at end of FR 7104 (USFS, primitive), Eightmile Campground (USFS)
Nearest food, drink, services: Cashmere

17 LEAVENWORTH
Freund Creek
☺☺☺

Distance	8.3 miles
Ride	Loop; singletrack, doubletrack
Duration	1 to 3 hours
Travel time	Wenatchee—30 minutes; Seattle—2.5 hours; Bellingham—3 hours
Hill factor	Healthy road and singletrack climb; 1,580-foot gain
Skill level	Intermediate
Season	Summer, fall
Maps	Green Trails: Leavenworth
Users	Bicyclists, equestrians, hikers
More info	Wenatchee National Forest, Leavenworth District, 509-548-6977

Climbing the ridge between Freund Creek and its southern tributary

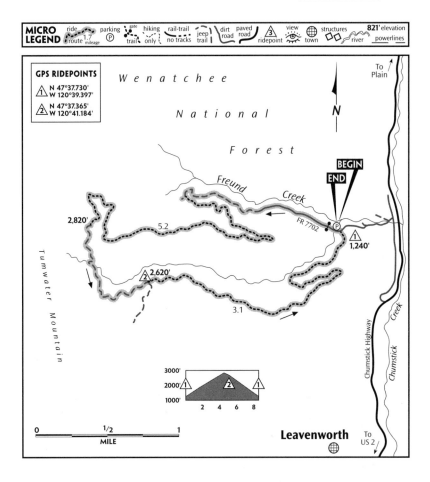

Prelude

This short ditty of a ride is a favorite of Leavenworth locals. Like the locals, you can easily add six miles to the route by beginning the ride from the ranger station in Leavenworth and following the directions in To Get There, below. The zippy singletrack belies the fact that most of the route follows an ancient roadbed, an excellent road-to-trails example. The views of Leavenworth from the ridge top are nice, but the signature of this ride has to be the mini-berm. Just hold on tight.

To Get There

Start your odometer at the Leavenworth Ranger Station on US Highway 2 in Leavenworth. Proceed east on US 2 for about one block, then turn left on State Route 209, the Chumstick Highway, toward Plain. At 1.9 miles, just before passing under the railroad bridge over the highway, turn left. The road immediately bends to the right and parallels Chumstick Highway. At 2.5 miles, turn left onto a dirt road, Forest Road 7702 (Freund Canyon Road). At 2.6 miles, bear left (not into the private drive). Pass through the Friendly Creek Tree Farm. At 2.8 miles, take the left fork. At 3 miles, still on FR 7702, reach a gate, and park.

The Ride

From the gate on FR 7702, pedal up the old dirt road. When the road seems to end at **1.4** miles, hike around a large berm to the left (don't climb up to the big slash pile) and find a trail. The singletrack, all that remains of FR 7702, switchbacks up the high ridge that separates the two forks of Freund Creek. Along the ridge top, there are views of Leavenworth and the Chumstick Valley. The trail continues a healthy ascent up the north slope of the ridge.

At **4.5** miles, the trail rounds a corner, widens to become a double-track, and begins descending. Cross the south fork of Freund Creek. Reach a fork, **5.2** miles, and bear left. The way becomes a narrow trail again and follows the course of an old road. The smooth, solid tread and consistent grade make for fast, fun riding; the mini-berms keep it interesting and don't always let you keep the rubber on the dirt. At **8.2** miles, the singletrack ends at FR 7702: Turn left, pedal a few rotations, and reach the gate to complete the loop at **8.3** miles.

Gazetteer

Nearby camping: Eightmile Campground (USFS), Lake Wenatchee State Park
Nearest food, drink, services: Leavenworth

18

Nason Ridge

✹✹✹✹

Distance	12 miles
Ride	Out & Back; singletrack; views
Duration	2 to 4 hours
Travel time	Wenatchee—1 hour; Seattle—2 hours; Bellingham—2.5 hours
Hill factor	Strenuous climb, some walking; 3,200-foot gain
Skill level	Intermediate
Season	Late summer, fall
Maps	Green Trails: Wenatchee Lake, Plain
Users	Bicyclists, equestrians, hikers, motorcyclists
More info	Wenatchee National Forest, Lake Wenatchee District (Leavenworth), 509-763-3103

Up Nason Ridge on Trail 1583

Prelude

The climb up Nason Ridge can be gritty and torturous if you haven't put in enough training time. But the excellent views from the top and the enjoyable descent are worth the effort for those who have. The last time I rode up Nason Ridge, the rainy, overcast day obscured most of the views, including those into Glacier Peak Wilderness. Some of the descent is switchbacked and relatively slow, but the lower section is fairly straight, and high speeds can annoy other trail users. Don't be a trail bully.

To Get There

Take US Highway 2 to its junction with State Route 207 at the town of Coles Corner (about 16 miles west of Leavenworth and 20 miles east of Stevens Pass). Turn north on SR 207 and zero out your odometer. At 3.7 miles, turn left onto Cedar Brae toward Nason Creek Campground. At 4 miles, turn left, staying on Cedar Brae. At 4.3 miles, turn left on Kahler Drive. Take the right fork at 4.5 miles, then at 4.6 miles find Nason Creek trailhead parking on the right.

The Ride

From the trailhead, pedal out Nason Creek Trail 1583. For the first quarter mile, the root-strewn singletrack noodles through the dark, big-tree lowlands near the east end of Lake Wenatchee. Soon, though, you begin a tough ascent up Nason Ridge. The climb is relentless, but after the **2**-mile mark, views of Lake Wenatchee and Fish Lake can be snatched through the trees, easing the pain. At **2.6** miles, there is a big intersection of three roads and two trails: Bear right, following the "Trail" signs up an old jeep track.

After several sandy switchbacks, the "Trail" is still a narrow, rutted jeep track. Crest a knoll at **3.2** miles, and descend for a short distance. Begin climbing again just as the jeep track narrows to become a single-track. From here, the trail switchbacks steeply up the eastern slope of the ridge toward Round Mountain. After a long, grinding climb, reach a fork at the eastern point of Round Mountain, **6** miles. Turn around here and coast back to the trailhead to complete the loop, **12** miles. **WHOA!** Watch for other trail users during the descent.

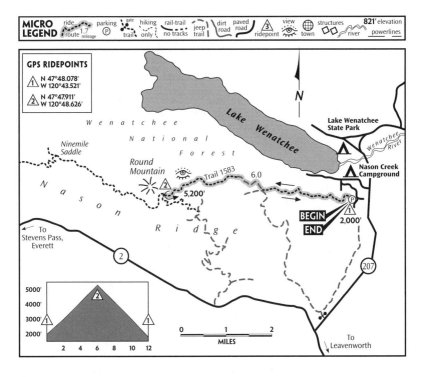

Option

From the fork in the trail at the eastern point of Round Mountain, bear right, hike up a series of tight switchbacks, then swing around the south side of the mountain. From here, let the truly awesome views of the Nason Creek Valley to the south and the White River Valley and Glacier Peak Wilderness to the north carry you west along the rugged Nason Ridge Trail. Ride 2.8 miles farther and reach a perch high above Ninemile Saddle. The trail drops precipitously down to the saddle, but I suggest turning around here to make this Out & Back ride 17.6 miles. You may want to stash your bike at the high perch, walk down to Ninemile Saddle, and then hike up to Alpine Lookout, 0.8 mile farther.

Gazetteer

Nearby camping: Nason Creek Campground (USFS), Lake Wenatchee State Park
Nearest food, drink, services: Plain

19 Chikamin Creek

☺☺☺

Distance	19.8 miles
Ride	Loop; singletrack, dirt road
Duration	3 to 5 hours
Travel time	Wenatchee—1 hour; Seattle—2 hours; Bellingham—2.5 hours
Hill factor	Healthy climb, some steep sections; 1,720-foot gain
Skill level	Intermediate
Season	Late summer, fall
Maps	Green Trails: Plain
Users	Bicyclists, equestrians, hikers, motorcyclists
More info	Wenatchee National Forest, Lake Wenatchee District (Leavenworth), 509-763-3103

Prelude

Like a mini-version of the Chikamin Ridge Epic, the Chikamin Creek loop has sections of challenging singletrack and excellent descents, but not

the views or utter exhaustion of its epic cousin. To make this ride more challenging, ride up Minnow Ridge Trail from Chikamin Creek trailhead, exchanging three and a quarter miles of dirt-road climbing for three and a half miles of singletrack climbing. I rode this on a hot August day and was happy to have the constant tree cover provided by the robust Chikamin Creek forest.

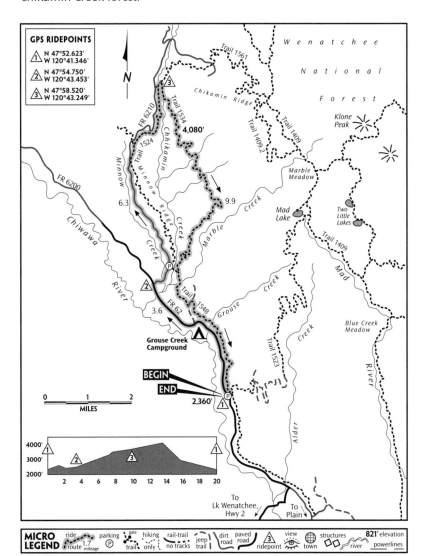

To Get There

Take US Highway 2 to its junction with State Route 207 at the town of Coles Corner (about 16 miles west of Leavenworth and 20 miles east of Stevens Pass). Turn north on SR 207 and set your odometer to zero. At 4.6 miles, just after crossing the Wenatchee River, turn right on Chiwawa Loop Road. At 5 miles, bear right again, then at 5.9 miles reach a fork and turn left on Meadow Creek Road (toward Chiwawa Valley). This road becomes Forest Road 62, which is paved. Soon after crossing Chiwawa River, FR 62 (aka Chiwawa River Road) veers to the left and parallels the river. At 12.4 miles, find Alder Ridge trailhead parking area on the right.

The Ride

From the trailhead parking area, ride back out to FR 62, turn right, and ride up the paved road. After a gentle climb, descend past Grouse Creek Campground, **2.2** miles. Continue up the paved road. At **3.6** miles, turn right onto FR 6210, which is dirt, and pedal north. Pass Chikamin Creek trailhead on the right at **4.1** miles. From here, the road heads up and the climbing becomes more arduous. At **7.1** miles, an unmarked trail (Minnow Ridge Trail 1524) kisses FR 6210 on the right: Hop on the trail here and continue riding north. At **7.3** miles, reach a fork and bear right. From here the trail cuts a fast traverse through the thick Chikamin Creek forest. At **9.7** miles, bear right at a fork and drop to the creek.

After crossing Chikamin Creek at **9.9** miles, the trail divides: Turn right on Chikamin Creek Trail 1534. The trail makes a gradual, traversing climb up the western flank of the Entiat Mountains, rolling and swelling in and out of numerous Chikamin Creek tributaries. At **13.7** miles, reach the high point and begin a fast—though technical—descent. Watch for roots and rocks. The steep grade eases and the trail smooths out. At **15.8** miles, reach a fork: Bear left on Lower Chiwawa Trail 1548. From the fork, the trail noodles southward through a heavy fir forest. At **17.5** miles, reach a dirt road and turn left. After a few pedal rotations, find the trail continuing on the right. After numerous ups and downs, arrive at the Alder Creek trailhead to complete the loop, **19.8** miles.

Gazetteer

Nearby camping: Grouse Creek Campground (USFS, primitive), Lake Wenatchee State Park
Nearest food, drink, services: Plain

20

LAKE WENATCHEE
Chikamin Ridge Epic
✿✿✿✿✿

Distance	33.7 miles
Ride	Loop; singletrack, dirt road; views
Duration	5 to 9 hours
Travel time	Wenatchee—1 hour; Seattle—2 hours; Bellingham—2.5 hours
Hill factor	Long, grueling climb, some hike-a-bike; 4,100-foot gain
Skill level	Advanced
Season	Late summer, fall
Maps	Green Trails: Plain
Users	Bicyclists, equestrians, hikers, motorcyclists
More info	Wenatchee National Forest, Lake Wenatchee District (Leavenworth), 509-763-3103

Prelude

This epic rates way up there; for me, it's a once-a-year ride at minimum. In spite of the 4,100-foot climb and extended distance of this loop, strong riders will be rewarded by the smooth trail and even grades that require less than one-quarter mile of walking over the entire thirty-two

High meadow near the headwaters of Alder Creek

miles. But that's only for really strong riders. Many cyclists will hike-a-bike up several series of switchbacks, though more due to exhaustion than steep grades or technical challenges. The views from the top of the Entiat Mountains are fantastic, but the beautiful subalpine meadows between the top of Chikamin Ridge and Mad Lake are the real treat of this ride. These trails are closed seasonally, usually opening in mid-July, so call ahead for current conditions.

To Get There

Take US Highway 2 to its junction with State Route 207 at the town of Coles Corner (about 16 miles west of Leavenworth and 20 miles east of Stevens Pass). Turn north on SR 207 and set your odometer to zero. At 4.6 miles, just after crossing the Wenatchee River, turn right on Chiwawa Loop Road. At 5 miles, bear right again, then at 5.9 miles reach a fork and turn left on Meadow Creek Road (toward Chiwawa Valley). This road becomes Forest Road 62, which is paved. Soon after crossing Chiwawa River, FR 62 (aka Chiwawa River Road) veers to the left and parallels the river. At 12.4 miles, find Alder Ridge trailhead parking area on the right.

The Ride

From the trailhead parking area, ride back out to FR 62, turn right, and ride up the paved road. The gentle grade makes a good warm-up for the tough singletrack climbing ahead. Pass Grouse Creek Campground on the left, at **2.2** miles. Continue up the main road. At **3.6** miles, turn right onto FR 6210, which is dirt, and pedal north. Pass Chikamin Creek trailhead on the right at **4.1** miles. From here, the road heads up, requiring several gear changes. At **7.1** miles, an unmarked trail (Minnow Ridge Trail 1524) kisses FR 6210 on the right: Hop on the trail here and continue north. Reach a fork at **7.3** miles and bear right, then slice a fast traverse, leaving Minnow Ridge for the dark forest near Chikamin Creek. At **9.7** miles, bear right at the fork and drop to the creek.

Immediately after crossing Chikamin Creek, **9.9** miles, the trail divides: Turn left on Chikamin Tie Trail 1561. From here, the trail winds and switchbacks around the northwest side of Chikamin Ridge. Cement pavers have been embedded in the trail around most of the switchbacks to prevent erosion. The great traction provided by these pavers, combined with excellent trail engineering and construction, allow strong riders to grind up nearly 3,000 feet over the next six miles. Maybe the

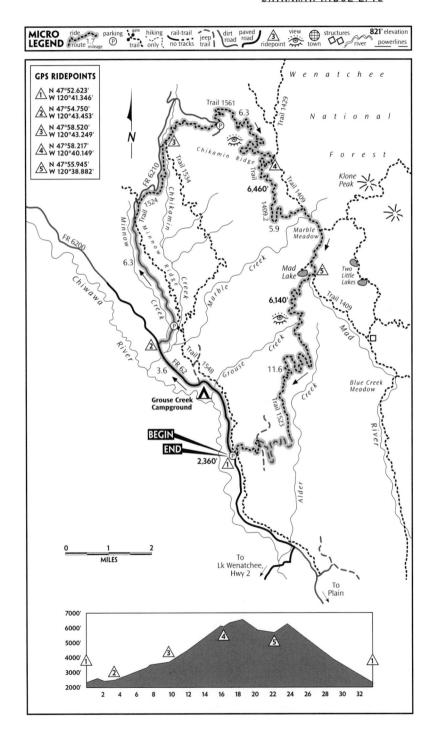

trail was built too well, because I found myself praying for a steep section so I could get off and walk for a while. The trail emerges from the forest, then at **12** miles crosses FR 6210. Continue up Chikamin Tie Trail 1561. After a couple of switchbacks, traverse back into a shaded forest and start climbing again. The trail rises into the subalpine forest of the Entiat Mountains. After cutting past the enormous rockfall that defines the northeast edge of Chikamin Ridge, reach the crest of the ridge at **15.9** miles.

From the crest, noodle through a scattered forest. Ignore Shetipo Trail 1429 back on the left, then arrive at a T, **16.2** miles. Turn right on Pond Camp Tie Trail 1409.2 (sung to the tune of "Camp Town Races"), and switchback up the ridge to a knoll. The knoll extends south, and the trail follows, rolling and swelling to the ride's high point at **18.5** miles. Fly down a number of quick twists and turns to a T, **20.1** miles, at Mad River Trail 1409.1. Turn right, riding down the wide, root-strewn, heavily used Mad River Trail, past Marble Meadow. Reach a fork and bear right, continuing south toward Mad Lake. Ignore the trail to Mad Lake on the right at **21.8** miles. When the trail divides at **22.1** miles, turn right on Alder Ridge Trail 1523 and begin climbing again.

The trail ascends out of the Upper Mad River basin. The climb is rigorous, but it's the last climb of the day. At **23.4** miles, the trail levels and noodles across a high meadow. After a short descent, **23.9** miles, find a spectacular vista that offers views west to Glacier Peak and south to the Stuart Range. From the viewpoint, the remainder of the route—down Alder Ridge to the trailhead at Chiwawa River 3,800 feet below—can be traced with your finger. Put on your windbreaker, eat your cookies, and get ready for nearly ten miles of switchback practice. After a long, corkscrewing downhill, reach a dirt road and bear right, **29.3** miles. At **29.4** miles, regain Alder Ridge Trail 1523 on the right. The trail widens, then, at **30.2** miles, follows a dirt road. Reach a T at **32.5** miles: Rather than turning, find the singletrack that continues straight ahead. At **33.4** miles, the trail crosses a dirt road. At **33.7** miles, arrive at Alder Creek trailhead to complete the loop.

Gazetteer

Nearby camping: Grouse Creek Campground (USFS, primitive), Lake Wenatchee State Park

Nearest food, drink, services: Plain

21

Minnow Ridge

☼☼☼

Distance	15.5 miles
Ride	Loop; singletrack, dirt road, paved road
Duration	2 to 4 hours
Travel time	Wenatchee—1 hour; Seattle—2 hours; Bellingham—2.5 hours
Hill factor	Moderate dirt-road climb; 1,100-foot gain
Skill level	Intermediate
Season	Summer, fall
Maps	Green Trails: Plain
Users	Bicyclists, equestrians, hikers, motorcyclists
More info	Wenatchee National Forest, Lake Wenatchee District (Leavenworth), 509-763-3103

Prelude

Not a particularly strenuous loop, Minnow Ridge offers a zippy, winding, not-too-technical descent down the narrow ridge. Short climbs during the descent keep you honest. To begin the ride, the climb up forest service roads is relatively easy, except for the last few miles, which are somewhat steep. You can combine this ride with Lower Chiwawa Trail (Ride 22) to create a longer outing. Check out the Green Trails map for other variations.

To Get There

Take US Highway 2 to its junction with State Route 207 at the town of Coles Corner (about 16 miles west of Leavenworth and 20 miles east of Stevens Pass). Turn north on SR 207 and set your odometer to zero. At 4.6 miles, just after crossing the Wenatchee River, turn right on Chiwawa Loop Road. At 5 miles, bear right again, then at 5.9 miles, reach a fork and turn left on Meadow Creek Road (toward Chiwawa Valley). This road becomes Forest Road 62, which is paved. Soon after crossing Chiwawa River, FR 62 (aka Chiwawa River Road) veers to the left and parallels the river. At 12.4 miles, find Alder Ridge trailhead parking area on the right.

The Ride

From the trailhead parking area, ride back out to FR 62, turn right, and ride up the paved road. After a gentle climb, descend past Grouse Creek Campground, **2.2** miles. Continue up the paved road. At **3.6** miles, turn right onto FR 6210, which is dirt, and pedal north. Pass Chikamin Creek trailhead on the right at **4.1** miles. From here, the road heads up and the climbing becomes more arduous. At **7.1** miles, an unmarked trail (Minnow Ridge Trail 1524) kisses FR 6210 on the right. Just around the corner, at the **7.3**-mile mark, a trail crosses FR 6210. Take a hard right on the wide trail. At **7.5** miles, reach a fork and bear right on Minnow Ridge Trail 1524.

From here, the trail heads due south, following the top of the narrow ridge squeezed between Minnow and Chikamin Creeks. After a long, twisting descent to the south end of the ridge, reach a fork and bear left, **11** miles. At **11.5** miles, arrive at a fork and turn right on Lower Chiwawa Trail 1548. From the fork, the trail noodles southward through a heavy fir forest. At **13.2** miles, reach a dirt road and turn left. After a few pedal

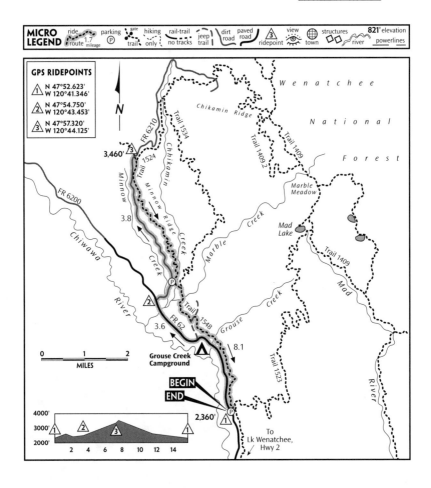

rotations, find the trail continuing on the right. After a few more rolls and swells, arrive at the Alder Creek trailhead to complete the loop, **15.5** miles.

Gazetteer

Nearby camping: Grouse Creek Campground (USFS, primitive), Lake Wenatchee State Park

Nearest food, drink, services: Plain

LAKE WENATCHEE

22 Lower Chiwawa Trail

☺☺☺

Distance	12.8 miles
Ride	Loop; singletrack, dirt road, paved road
Duration	2 to 3 hours
Travel time	Wenatchee—1 hour; Seattle—2 hours; Bellingham—2.5 hours
Hill factor	Rolling with a couple steep climbs; 160-foot gain
Skill level	Intermediate
Season	Summer, fall
Maps	Green Trails: Plain
Users	Bicyclists, equestrians, hikers, motorcyclists
More info	Wenatchee National Forest, Lake Wenatchee District (Leavenworth), 509-763-3103

Prelude

The Lower Chiwawa Trail defines the term "corkscrew": to ride down a steep, winding, twisting trail. This roller-coaster ride tosses in numerous corkscrews along with several sharp climbs. It's relatively easy and action-packed. Combine it with Minnow Ridge (Ride 21) to create a longer loop. My only grievance was the dirt-stale peanut butter energy bar I ate that day, but even this culinary low point didn't sour the ride for me.

To Get There

Take US Highway 2 to its junction with State Route 207 at the town of Coles Corner (about 16 miles

Snack break on the Lower Chiwawa Trail

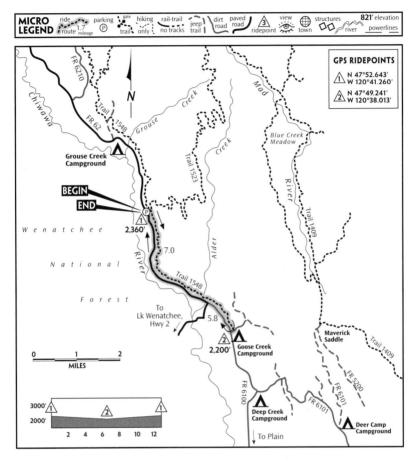

west of Leavenworth and 20 miles east of Stevens Pass). Turn north on SR 207 and set your odometer to zero. At 4.6 miles, just after crossing the Wenatchee River, turn right on Chiwawa Loop Road. At 5 miles, bear right again, then at 5.9 miles reach a fork and turn left on Meadow Creek Road (toward Chiwawa Valley). This road becomes Forest Road 62, which is paved. Soon after crossing Chiwawa River, FR 62 (aka Chiwawa River Road) veers to the left and parallels the river. At 12.4 miles, find Alder Ridge trailhead parking area on the right and park.

The Ride

Three trails exit from Alder Ridge trailhead. Take the one on the right, Lower Chiwawa Trail 1548, and head south. At **0.1** mile, cross FR 6209 (just to the east of paved FR 62) and continue down the trail. The trail climbs a bit, and then begins the raucous corkscrewing. At **3.7** miles, cross a dirt road; stay on the main trail. Cross another dirt road at **4** miles. Ignore a spur trail on the right at **4.3** miles. Reach a fork at **4.9** miles and bear left, continuing down Trail 1548 (Goose Creek Campground is to the right). Ignore several trails on the right that spur down to the campground. At **5.2** miles, cross a dirt road. From here, the trail climbs steadily to the **5.5**-mile point, then descends. Cross another dirt road at **6.8** miles. The trail ends at a dirt road next to Deep Creek Campground, **7** miles. At the end of the trail, turn right onto FR 6100. Stay on the main road, ignoring spurs, as you head north. Pass by Goose Creek Campground. At **9.7** miles, bear to the left and meet FR 62, which is paved. Turn right on FR 62 and pedal up to the Alder Creek trailhead to complete the loop, **12.8** miles.

Gazetteer

Nearby camping: Deep Creek Campground (USFS, primitive), Lake Wenatchee State Park

Nearest food, drink, services: Plain

23 Mad Lake

◎◎◎

Distance	18 miles
Ride	Out & Back; singletrack; views
Duration	3 to 4 hours
Travel time	Wenatchee—1.5 hours; Seattle—2.5 hours; Bellingham—3 hours
Hill factor	Sustained, difficult ascent; 1,440-foot gain
Skill level	Intermediate
Season	Late summer, fall
Maps	Green Trails: Plain
Users	Bicyclists, equestrians, hikers, motorcyclists
More info	Wenatchee National Forest, Entiat District, 509-784-1511

Mad River at Blue Creek Meadow

Prelude

High meadows, sweet-flowing creeks, and mountain-bike trails galore—what could be better? The trip up to Mad Lake is really lovely and should be high on every serious mountain biker's To Do list. (Ignore the fact that a lovely trip on a To Do list is something of a contradiction.) If you're running for your scheduler now, try to ride this trail midweek, because it's only open between mid-July and early October, and hot summer weekends can be crowded. (Each year the closure dates are different, so call ahead for current conditions and restrictions.) Be aware that this trail system is heavily used by equestrians and motorcyclists.

To Get There

Take US Highway 2 to its junction with State Route 207 at the town of Coles Corner (about 16 miles west of Leavenworth and 20 miles east of Stevens Pass). Turn north on SR 207 and set your odometer to zero. At 4.6 miles, just after crossing the Wenatchee River, turn right on Chiwawa Valley Road. At 5 miles, bear right again. Stay on Chiwawa Valley Road. Cross the Chiwawa River at 9.6 miles. At 10 miles, just as the road bends to the right around Thousand Trails Campground, take a hard left onto Forest Road 6100. At 11.7 miles, reach a T and turn right onto FR 6101. Stay on FR 6101. At Deer Camp Campground, 15 miles, turn left, continuing up FR 6101 toward Mad River Trail. After a hair-raising traverse, reach Maverick Saddle at 17.8 miles. Park near the hairpin turn.

The Ride

From the hairpin turn at Maverick Saddle, turn left and ride down the narrow road, following the signs to "Mad River Trail." At **0.2** mile, reach a second trailhead. Bear left and ascend Upper Mad River Trail 1409.1 (Lower Mad River Trail 1409 originates from the same trailhead). The trail climbs at a moderate grade. At **1.5** miles, pass Hi Yu Trail 1403 on the left. Cross Mad River and at **1.7** miles, pass Jimmy Creek Trail 1419 on the right. Again, continue straight on Trail 1409.1, which is wide, though root-strewn and somewhat technical. Around **3.4** miles, the trail levels and crosses a beautiful meadow. Bypass the trail to Lost Lake (1421) at **3.7** miles.

At **5** miles, pass Trail 1415 on the right (which heads up Whistling Pig Creek). Continue up the Upper Mad River Trail. The Upper Mad River basin widens and reveals Blue Creek Meadow on the left at around **5.7** miles.

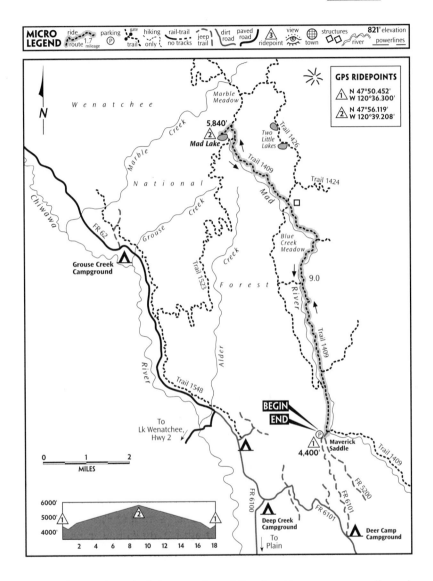

MICRO LEGEND: ride route 1.7 mileage · parking ⓟ · gate · hiking trail · rail-trail no tracks · jeep trail · dirt road · paved road · 3 ridepoint · view · town · structures · 821' elevation · river · powerlines

GPS RIDEPOINTS
△1 N 47°50.452'
W 120°36.300'
△2 N 47°56.119'
W 120°39.208'

Reach the north end of the meadow, **6.3** miles, then cross a small creek and arrive at a fork. Notice the old guard station off to the right. Ignore the trail to Lost Lake on the left, then, almost immediately, pass Blue Creek Trail 1426 on the right; continue up the wide, heavily used Upper Mad River Trail toward Mad Lake. At **8.3** miles, pass Trail 1523 on the left. At the next fork, **8.6** miles, turn left on Mad Lake Trail 1406. Reach Mad Lake at **9** miles. Turn around here and descend back to Maverick Saddle on the wide, fast, technical trail to complete the route, **18** miles.

Option

You can add more climbing, a narrow, winding trail, and three miles to this route by continuing north on Upper Mad River Trail 1409.1. At Marble Meadow, turn right on Trail 1425, climb to a fork, and turn right on Trail 1426. After a long, winding, somewhat technical descent (and a climb or two) past Two Little Lakes (Louise and Ann), reach a fork and bear right. Reach the old guard station and bear left down Upper Mad River Trail 1409.1. Descend to Maverick Saddle.

Gazetteer

Nearby camping: Deep Creek Campground (USFS, primitive), Lake Wenatchee State Park
Nearest food, drink, services: Plain

24 Lower Mad River Trail

⊕⊕⊕

Distance	15.6 miles
Ride	One Way (2-hour shuttle); singletrack
Duration	2 to 5 hours
Travel time	Wenatchee—1.5 hours; Seattle—2.5 hours; Bellingham—3 hours
Hill factor	Long, technical descent, some hike-a-bike; 2,720-foot loss
Skill level	Advanced
Season	Late summer, fall
Maps	Green Trails: Plain, Brief
Users	Bicyclists, equestrians, hikers, motorcyclists
More info	Wenatchee National Forest, Entiat District, 509-784-1511

Rebirth of a charred forest along Lower Mad River

Prelude

The Lower Mad River Trail is the only one-way ride described in this book. Strong riders could ride this as an Out & Back, beginning from Pine Flat Campground (the trail is technically demanding, so leave plenty of time). For the one-wayers: The long shuttle just means that you'll have to find someone who really loves you. Other than the beautiful, winding river and striking canyon, this route primarily features an up-close look at the devastating 1994 Tyee Creek Fire. Blackened trees, stumps, and charred hillsides spot the river valley as well as the ridges above. When I rode this trail I had just seen *The Edge,* a movie in which a grizzly bear figures prominently, so in my mind every blackened stump was a crouching bear. Finally, I decided to ignore the black apparitions—but what if the one I ignored was the *real* bear? Just past the four-mile point, the trail is unstable and susceptible to washing out, so call the ranger station to inquire about current conditions.

To Get There

Take US Highway 2 to its junction with State Route 207 at the town of Coles Corner (about 16 miles west of Leavenworth and 20 miles east of Stevens Pass). Turn north on SR 207 and set your odometer to zero. At 4.6 miles, just after crossing the Wenatchee River, turn right on Chiwawa Valley Road. At 5 miles, bear right again. Stay on Chiwawa Valley Road. Cross the Chiwawa River at 9.6 miles. At 10 miles, just as the road bends to the right around Thousand Trails Campground, take a hard left onto Forest Road 6100. At 11.7 miles, reach a T and turn right onto FR 6101. Stay on FR 6101. At Deer Camp Campground, 15 miles, turn left and continue up FR 6101 toward Mad River Trail. After a hair-raising traverse, reach Maverick Saddle at 17.8 miles. Park near the hairpin turn.

The Ride

From the hairpin turn at Maverick Saddle, turn left and ride down the narrow road, following the signs to "Mad River Trail." At **0.2** mile, reach a second trailhead. Turn right and pedal down Lower Mad River Trail 1409 (Upper Mad River Trail 1409.1 originates from the same trailhead). Drop down the wide trail, passing a spur and a campsite on the left, to Mad River at **0.7** mile. Cross the river and continue the descent, at times uneven and technical. Follow the frenetically winding river to the southeast. At a fork, **4** miles, stay to the right, toward Pine Flats Campground.

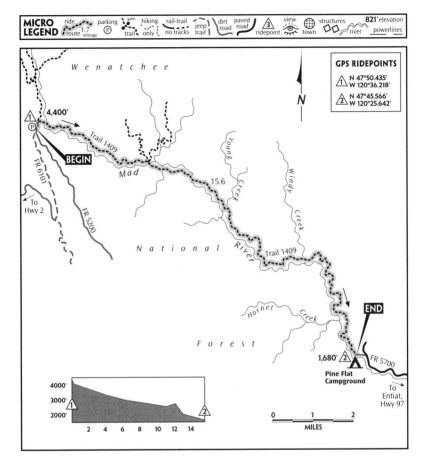

ride route 1.7 mileage | parking P | gate trail | hiking only | rail-trail no tracks | jeep trail | dirt road | paved road | 3 ridepoint | view | structures | town | river | 821' elevation powerlines

GPS RIDEPOINTS

⚠️1 N 47°50.435'
W 120°36.218'

⚠️2 N 47°45.566'
W 120°25.642'

Soon after the fork, the trail switchbacks down, crosses the river, and runs along the southern bank for a while. **WHOA!** Several small washouts obstruct the route; cross them with care. This section may be washed out or rerouted in the future; call ahead for current conditions.

The trail recrosses the river and continues the sometimes rough, sometime smooth and fast descent along the river. The devastation of the 1994 Tyee Creek Fire becomes more apparent: an old fire-scarred pine, a charred stump, a stand of black, branchless trees. Around the edges, new green growth takes hold and the experience is both startling and affirming. Some sections of the trail may seem less maintained because burned trees continue to fall across the trail, several years after the fire. Cross Young Creek at **7** miles. When you reach a fork at **9.4** miles, stay to the right. Bear right again a few pedal strokes farther to remain on Lower Mad River Trail 1409. As the valley closes to form a canyon, the trail climbs up and away from the river. Reach a crest at **11.2** miles, then switchback down a very steep, rocky slope to the river again. Follow the rough, riverside trail through a craggy canyon. Pass a campsite on the right at **14.1** miles. At **15.6** miles, reach Pine Flats Campground to complete the one-way ride.

Gazetteer

Nearby camping: Deep Creek Campground (USFS, primitive), Lake Wenatchee State Park
Nearest food, drink, services: Plain

25 Entiat River

◉◉

Distance	8.2 miles
Ride	Out & Back; singletrack; views
Duration	1 to 2 hours
Travel time	Wenatchee—1.5 hours; Seattle—4.5 hours
Hill factor	Easy to moderate climb; 650-foot gain
Skill level	Intermediate
Season	Late summer, fall
Maps	Green Trails: Lucerne
Users	Bicyclists, equestrians, hikers, motorcyclists
More info	Wenatchee National Forest, Entiat District, 509-784-1511

Bridge over Entiat River

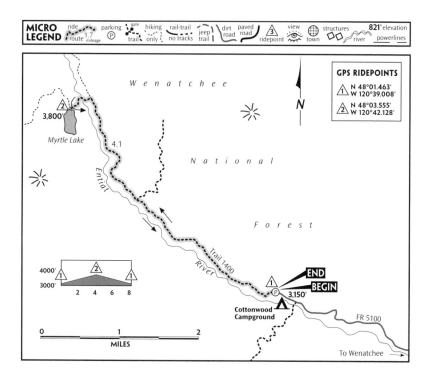

Prelude

Riding along the main fork of the Entiat River is a joy. The easy climb and smooth, compact trail make the cycling experience pleasant. The Douglas fir forest near the ride's beginning gives way to a more open, subalpine forest to the north, affording views of the surrounding craggy peaks near the Glacier Peak Wilderness boundary. Myrtle Lake is a lovely spot for picnicking or just lounging around in the hot August sun. Though this great trail continues into the wilderness area, bicycles are excluded, so be sure to only go as far as the lake.

To Get There

From Wenatchee, travel north on Alternate US Highway 97 up the west side of Lake Entiat. Before reaching the town of Entiat, turn left on Entiat River Road and start your odometer. Pass through the hamlet of Ardenvoir at 9.9 miles. Farther north, Entiat River Road becomes Forest Road 51. Pass Lake Creek Campground on the left at 28.8 miles, then pass Lake Creek trailhead at 28.9 miles. Continue up FR 51, which becomes FR

5100 after the road turns to dirt at 34 miles. At 35 miles, bear left, staying on FR 5100. Continue up FR 5100, past Cottonwood Guard Station and Campground, both on the left. FR 5100 ends at the trailhead for Entiat River Trail 1400, 39.2 miles.

The Ride

From the trailhead, pedal out Entiat River Trail 1400, gradually ascending through old growth. The smooth, well-graded trail follows the river north toward Myrtle Lake, as well as Glacier Peak Wilderness beyond. At around the **2**-mile mark, the heavy forest opens a bit, revealing several stunning nearby peaks. At **2.2** miles, ignore Trail 1435 on the right: Continue straight up Trail 1400. When you reach a fork at **3.7** miles, turn left on Cow Creek Meadows Trail 1404 (from this point north, Entiat River Trail is closed to bicycles). Trail 1404

Myrtle Lake

soon crosses the Entiat River. At **4.1** miles, reach Myrtle Lake. After soaking in the scenery, turn around and pedal back to the trailhead to complete the ride, **8.2** miles.

Gazetteer

Nearby camping: Cottonwood Campground (USFS), Silver Falls Campground (USFS), Lake Creek Campground (USFS)
Nearest food, drink, services: Entiat

26 North Fork Entiat River

⊛⊛⊛

Distance	12.8 miles
Ride	Out & Back; singletrack
Duration	2 to 4 hours
Travel time	Wenatchee—1.5 hours; Seattle—4.5 hours
Hill factor	Rough, difficult climb, some hike-a-bike; 1,280-foot gain
Skill level	Advanced
Season	Summer, fall
Maps	Green Trails: Lucerne
Users	Bicyclists, equestrians, hikers
More info	Wenatchee National Forest, Entiat District, 509-784-1511

Crossing Pyramid Creek

Prelude

With a rough and bumpy tread and numerous technical challenges, this is no place for the first-time mountain biker, despite the relatively short distance and modest elevation gain. This ride can function as a bike-and-hike to Fern Lake or up into the Chelan Mountains. Of course, nothing's wrong with a simple Out & Back through a nice forest. This trail is heavily used by equestrians, so watch your speed and be a courteous trail user.

To Get There

From Wenatchee, travel north on Alternate US Highway 97 up the west side of Lake Entiat. Before reaching the town of Entiat, turn left on Entiat River Road and start your odometer. Pass through the hamlet of Ardenvoir

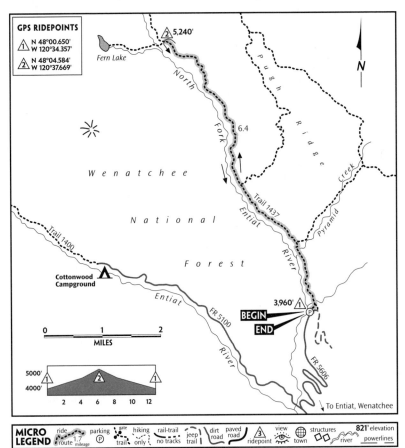

A technical section on Trail 1437

at 9.9 miles. Further north, Entiat River Road becomes Forest Road 51. Pass Lake Creek Campground on the left at 28.8 miles, then pass Lake Creek trailhead at 28.9 miles. At 34 miles, turn right on FR 5606, which is dirt. FR 5606 switchbacks up a steep hillside. At 36.6 miles, bear left at the fork. At 38.1 miles, find the North Fork Entiat River Trail 1437 trailhead on the left and park.

The Ride

From the trailhead, ride out North Fork Entiat River Trail 1437. After a few turns, ignore a trail on the right (which leads to an upper parking area) and continue on the main trail. Drop to a creek crossing, then slowly work your way up the singletrack that follows the river to the north. The trail is rough, hard, and chunky. At **1.2** miles, cross Pyramid Creek and continue up the knotted trail. At **1.3** miles, ignore a trail on the right. At times the trail is smooth and fast, but much of the trip travels over a ragged tread and past numerous technical challenges. At **2.8** miles, reach a fork and bear left. From here, Trail 1437 becomes steeper and at times punishing. At **6.4** miles, reach a fork. Turn around here and cruise back to the trailhead to complete the Out & Back, **12.8** miles.

Gazetteer

Nearby camping: Cottonwood Campground (USFS), Silver Falls Campground (USFS), Lake Creek Campground (USFS)
Nearest food, drink, services: Entiat

27 ENTIAT
Klone Peak
❀❀❀❀

Distance	27.2 miles
Ride	Loop; singletrack, dirt road; views
Duration	5 to 9 hours
Travel time	Wenatchee—1.5 hours; Seattle—4.5 hours
Hill factor	Long, strenuous climb, some hike-a-bike; 3,460-foot gain
Skill level	Advanced
Season	Late summer, fall
Maps	Green Trails: Plain; USFS: Entiat Ranger District
Users	Bicyclists, equestrians, hikers, motorcyclists
More info	Wenatchee National Forest, Entiat District, 509-784-1511

Prelude

We chomped into this ride, but it bit back. The beginning, a long, rigorous, 3,400-foot climb, is a hookybobber's dream. But in the scorching August heat, my attempts at hookybobbing—grabbing the back of your friend's bike for a tow—quickly ceased to be funny. The clock was ticking during the infinite series of switchbacks up to Klone Peak, during the photo time along the rocky slopes near the top, and while we lingered in the beautiful meadows of the Upper Mad River basin. The result: We rode the last several miles in pitch-dark, most of us concentrating hard to stay

Climbing the steep, rocky trail up the south slope of Klone Peak

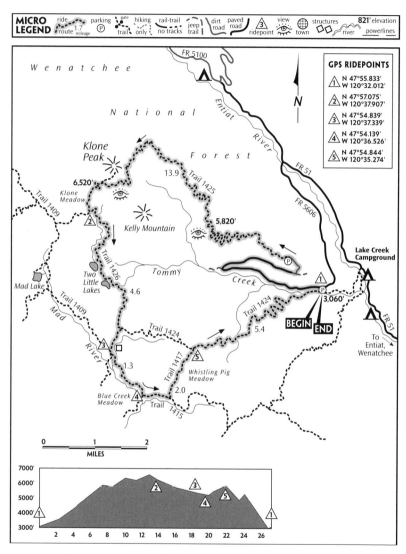

ride route 1.7 mileage | parking Ⓟ gate | hiking trail only | rail-trail no tracks | jeep trail | dirt road paved road | ③ ridepoint | view town | structures river | 821' elevation powerlines

GPS RIDEPOINTS

△1 N 47°55.833' W 120°32.012'
△2 N 47°57.075' W 120°37.907'
△3 N 47°54.839' W 120°37.339'
△4 N 47°54.139' W 120°36.526'
△5 N 47°54.844' W 120°35.274'

W e n a t c h e e

N a t i o n a l

F o r e s t

Klone Peak

6,520'
Klone Meadow

13.9 Trail 1425

Kelly Mountain

5,820'

Trail 1409

Trail 1426

Two Little Lakes

Mad Lake

T o m m y   *C r e e k*

4.6

Trail 1409

Mad River

Trail 1424

Trail 1424

5.4

3,060'

BEGIN END

Lake Creek Campground

To Entiat, Wenatchee

1.3

Trail 1417

Trail 1424

△5

Whistling Pig Meadow

Blue Creek Meadow

2.0

Trail 1415

FR 5100

FR 51

FR 5606

N

0   1   2
MILES

7000'
6000'
5000'
4000'
3000'
    2 4 6 8 10 12 14 16 18 20 22 24 26

on the trail, some of us walking. But one friend, blistering along in the dark, flew off the trail and crashed into the brush below. We looked down at the wreckage. "Are you hurt? What happened?" we asked. He said, "I was just checking out the stars." So much for concentrating on the trail. We compassed the loop, somewhat worse for wear, but enthralled by the brilliant stars. This loop is usually closed until mid-July, depending on the snowpack, so call the ranger station for current conditions.

To Get There

From Wenatchee, travel north on Alternate US Highway 97 up the west side of Lake Entiat. Before reaching the town of Entiat, turn left on Entiat River Road and start your odometer. Pass through the hamlet of Ardenvoir at 9.9 miles. Entiat River Road becomes Forest Road 51. Pass Lake Creek Campground on the left at 28.8 miles, then pass Lake Creek trailhead at 28.9 miles. At 31.9 miles, turn left on FR 5605, also paved. At 35 miles, turn left into the parking area for Middle Tommy Trail.

The Ride

From the trailhead parking area, ride back out to FR 5605, turn left, and pedal up the paved road, following the signs for Tommy Creek Trail. Stay on the paved road. After two long, uphill switchbacks, the road becomes gravel at **3.5** miles. Stay on the main road until it ends, **4.1** miles, at the trailhead for North Tommy Trail 1425. A wide dirt trail exits from the west side of the parking area. Take it and begin the merciless climb toward Klone Peak. The trail narrows to a singletrack at **4.4** miles, winding through a mixed pine and fir forest. The switchbacks are relentless. To prevent erosion, cement pavers have been embedded in the trail around many of the switchbacks. The pavers provide great traction, but your legs might find the endless series of steep, ridable switchbacks annoying.

After more switchbacks than you can count on your fingers and toes combined, crest the top of a high knoll, **7.4** miles. Rest on the rocks and admire the beautiful views of Kelly Mountain and the Tommy Creek drainage. From the top of the high knoll, the trail follows a ridge that swings northwest around Kelly Mountain. The next five miles are zippy, winding, switchbacky fun as the trail rides the roll and swell of the ridge top, through a light forest. Around the **12**-mile mark, the trail becomes steeper as it rounds the rocky southern face of Klone Peak. WHOA! Pass an adrenaline-pumping section of trail that tootles along the cliff between Klone Peak and Kelly Mountain. At **12.8** miles, reach a fork at the ride's high point and turn left (turn right to bag Klone Peak, which is a half mile and 300 feet of climbing beyond this point).

After descending a couple of technical switchbacks, noodle across Klone Meadow to a T at **13.9** miles. Turn left onto Blue Creek Trail 1426 toward Two Little Lakes. From here, enjoy an amazing, twisting, corkscrew descent that follows the trickling headwaters of Tommy Creek. WHOA! This trail is heavily used, as are the rest of the trails in the Upper Mad River basin, so watch out for other trail users. Lake Louise appears at **16** miles. Pass the trail to the lake on the right, then begin climbing a root-strewn trail. A little farther, pass Lake Ann and continue climbing. Soon, though, you'll be happy again, descending along Blue Creek to a fork at **18** miles. Turn right, continuing down Blue Creek Trail (a left turn here shaves one mile and some tough, technical climbing from the loop). At **18.5** miles, where there's a wood guard station on the left, reach Mad Lake Trail 1409. Bear left onto Trail 1409, then immediately bear left again, remaining on Mad Lake Trail. At **19.8** miles, after a fast cruise around the edge of Blue Creek Meadow, reach a fork and turn left on Tyee Ridge Trail 1415.

From here, the trail climbs steeply along Whistling Pig Creek. When you reach a fork at **20.5** miles, go left on Hunters Trail 1417, continuing the steep, technical climb. A break in the arduous ascent comes at around **21** miles as the trail noodles across Whistling Pig Meadow, the last and most unexpected meadow of the ride. At **21.8** miles, reach a T and turn right on Middle Tommy Trail 1424. After a few level turns, the trail switchbacks down into the heavily forested ravine of a Tommy Creek tributary. Across the creek, hike-a-bike up the eastern side of the ravine, the difficult but final climb of the ride. From the top, the trail again switchbacks steeply down, dropping 2,000 feet over the next three miles. When the hectic descent finally ends, ford Tommy Creek and climb a short distance to a fork at **27.1** miles. Bear left and climb to the trailhead to complete the loop, **27.2** miles.

Option

A slightly easier but equally scenic loop can be formed by turning right at the T at 13.9 miles. Take Trail 1425 to Mad River Trail 1409 and turn left. Follow Mad River Trail to the wood guard station and turn left again on Trail 1426. From here, take the first right onto Middle Tommy Trail 1424. Pick up the route described above at the 21.8-mile point as you pass Hunters Trail on the right. This version is less technical, comes with fewer climbs, and is about one mile shorter than the route described above.

Gazetteer

Nearby camping: Silver Falls Campground (USFS), Lake Creek Campground (USFS)
Nearest food, drink, services: Entiat

28

ENTIAT
Lake Creek
◎◎◎◎

Distance	28 miles
Ride	Loop; singletrack, dirt road; views
Duration	5 to 8 hours
Travel time	Wenatchee—1.5 hours; Seattle—4.5 hours
Hill factor	Long, strenuous climb, some hike-a-bike; 4,680-foot gain
Skill level	Advanced
Season	Late summer, fall
Maps	Green Trails: Plain, Brief; USFS: Entiat Ranger District
Users	Bicyclists, equestrians, hikers, motorcyclists
More info	Wenatchee National Forest, Entiat District, 509-784-1511

Prelude

This ride climbs up to nearly 7,000 feet, so call the ranger station to make sure the trail is clear of snow. Of course, I scouted this route at the end of the season, after the first snow had fallen, and it wasn't the snow that made it a difficult loop, but the huge amount of elevation gain and rough trail. I've heard, though, that if you hit this trail right, give the sun a couple of weeks to dry out the meadows and hillside and coax the wildflowers into bloom, Lake Creek basin is one of the more beautiful places on earth.

To Get There

From Wenatchee, travel north on Alternate US Highway 97 up the west side of Lake Entiat. Before reaching the town of Entiat, turn left on Entiat River Road and start your odometer. Pass through the hamlet of Arden-voir at 9.9 miles. Entiat River Road becomes Forest Road 51. At 28.8 miles, turn left into Lake Creek Campground. Park here.

The Ride

From Lake Creek Campground, which sits on a perch above the scenic Entiat River, ride up FR 51. After a few tire rotations up the paved road, pass the Lake Creek trailhead parking area on the left and Lake Creek Trail on the right. The easy warm-up complete, turn right on FR 5900, **1.1** miles. From here, the dirt road climbs fitfully as it zigzags up a massive ridge into the Chelan Mountains. Pass numerous lesser spur roads during the strenuous ascent. Pass Halfway Springs Campground at **4.3** miles, and continue climbing up FR 5900. The road gains the ridge top at around the **8**-mile point. From here, the road rolls and swells along the top of the ridge. When the road forks at Shady Pass Campground, **8.7** miles, turn right. FR 5900 swings west at this point, straddling the spine of the Chelan Mountains, about 5,000 feet above Lake Chelan to the north and 1,000 feet above the Lake Creek basin to the south. Stay on the main road.

   The ridge-top road continues rising and falling, finally rising toward Crescent Hill. At **13.2** miles, take a hard right onto FR 114. **WHOA!** This is an easy turn to miss. Climb up FR 114, bear to the right (don't go down to Handy Spring Campground), and reach the trailhead at **13.7** miles. Check out the spectacular views of Glacier Peak Wilderness to the north-west and the Sawtooth Mountains to the northeast. Devils Backbone

96

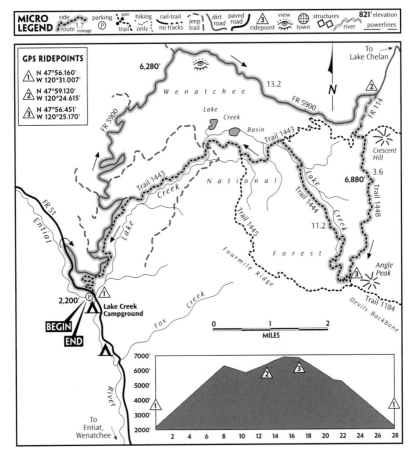

Trail 1448 takes off from here, climbing steeply. For the next three miles, the trail is wide and ragged, a leftover firebreak built during the cataclysmic 1994 Tyee Creek Fire. At **13.9** miles, the trail forks: Bear left. When the trail forks again at **14** miles, bear right and continue up the narrow ridge toward Angle Peak and Devils Backbone beyond. The rough ridge trail cuts up and down, forcing some hike-a-biking but offering many great views. At **16.8** miles, just before cresting Angle Peak, reach a fork: Turn right on Angle Peak Trail 1444.

From here, the rocky trail descends sharply, switchbacking off the high ridge. After the **17.6**-mile mark, the grade eases somewhat, and the trail follows the flow of Lake Creek into Lake Creek Basin. Cross the creek several times as you weave through a scattered pine forest. When the trail forks at **20.8** miles, turn left onto Lake Creek Trail 1443. From here, the trail climbs for a half mile, then spins around the south edge of the lovely basin. At **21.7** miles, ignore Trail 1445 on the left. From here, get ready to drop 2,500 feet over the next six miles. Cross a dirt road at **22.4** miles. The trail leaves the basin and drops into the Lake Creek valley. Stay on the main trail. At **23.9** miles, bear left as the trail runs along an old road for a stretch. Cross several more roads and jeep tracks. At **25.8** miles, the trail kisses FR 5900, then bends away from it. At **27.9** miles, the trail ends at FR 51. Turn left and ride back to Lake Creek Campground to complete the loop, **28** miles.

Gazetteer

Nearby camping: Silver Falls Campground (USFS), Lake Creek Campground (USFS)

Nearest food, drink, services: Entiat

29 CHELAN
Pot Peak Epic
✵✵✵✵✵

Distance	30.1 miles
Ride	Loop; singletrack, dirt road; views
Duration	6 to 10 hours
Travel time	Wenatchee—1 hour; Seattle—4 hours
Hill factor	Long dirt-road climb, lots of walking; 4,920-foot gain
Skill level	Advanced
Season	Late summer, fall
Maps	Green Trails: Brief; USFS: Entiat Ranger District
Users	Bicyclists, equestrians, hikers, motorcyclists
More info	Wenatchee National Forest, Chelan District, 509-682-2576

Headed toward Devils Backbone on Trail 1448 late in the season

Prelude

I guarantee that when you complete this ride, you will say it's the best singletrack descent you've ever done. That's a strong statement, and I know that there's lots of climbing, hike-a-biking, and out-and-out pushing required before you can test the claim, but you won't be disappointed. The smooth, compact-dirt trail from Devils Backbone past Pot Peak and down to Twenty-Five Mile Creek is more fun than you can imagine. To save your legs (and your senses), you may want to shuttle part or all of the dirt-road climb. Of course if you do, it no longer qualifies as an epic.

To Get There

From Wenatchee, travel north on Alternate US Highway 97 up the west side of the Columbia River. Past the town of Entiat, turn left on State Route 971 (Navarre Coulee Road) toward Lake Chelan State Park. After about 7 miles, turn left on South Lakeshore Drive and proceed north along Lake Chelan. Pass Twenty-Five Mile Creek State Park on your right. Soon after, turn left onto Shady Pass Road (Forest Road 5900) and set your odometer to zero. At 2.8 miles, the road forks: Turn left and drop down FR 8410, which is gravel. At 3.2 miles, reach tiny Ramona Campground on the right. Park here.

The Ride

From Ramona Campground, set in a tight wedge between two forks of Twenty-Five Mile Creek, ride back up FR 8410 toward Shady Pass Road. Let the climbing begin. At **0.5** mile, reach a fork and take a hard left on FR 5900, which is dirt. The road climbs west to Darby Draw, then begins the long series of switchbacks up to Grouse Mountain Campground. Pass FR 5903 on the left at **2.6** miles. Continue up the main road, catching occasional views of Lake Chelan to the east. At **6.2** miles, 2,600 feet above the starting point, pass by Grouse Mountain Campground on the right. Again, stay on the main road, ignoring lesser spurs and firebreaks.

From the campground, FR 5900 climbs steadily, marching up the high ridge between Lake Chelan and the Twenty-Five Mile Creek drainage. At **8.6** miles, pass a viewpoint and continue climbing. The road levels, then descends to Chesapeake Saddle, **11.2** miles. From the saddle, the road heads up again at a steep grade toward Crescent Hill. At **12.8** miles, roll over a high point; pass the road to Junior Point Campground on the left.

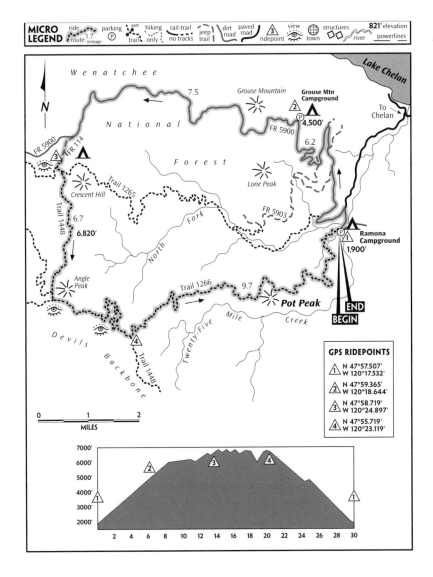

After a short descent, the road forks: Bear left on FR 114 toward Devils Backbone trailhead. Stay to the right (don't go down to Handy Spring Campground) and reach the trailhead at **13.7** miles. Check out the spectacular views of Glacier Peak Wilderness to the northwest and the Sawtooth Mountains to the northeast.

Devils Backbone Trail 1448 takes off, climbing steeply, from the trail-head. For the next three miles, the trail is wide and somewhat ragged, a leftover from fighting the cataclysmic 1994 Tyee Creek Fire. At **13.9** miles, the trail forks: Bear left. When the trail forks again at **14** miles, bear right and continue up the narrow ridge toward Angle Peak and Devils Backbone beyond. The wide, at times rough, ridge trail bucks up and down, offering many, many great views, as well as a little hike-a-biking. At **16.8** miles, reach a fork and bear left. Just up the trail, reach Angle Peak and another fork. Bear left, continuing on Trail 1448 toward Pot Peak Trail. From here, the trail cuts around the south flank of Angle Peak and out across a sheer, angular ridge—Devils Backbone. The trail remains rugged but ridable. At **18.3** miles, reach a fork and bear left. (To the right, find a scary viewpoint at the edge of a precipice. From the viewpoint, you can almost throw a rock across to the trail on the opposite side. Unfortunately, you can't ride that way.) Just after the fork, descend a few switchbacks and, quickly, the ridability ends. Hike about three-quarters of a mile up an incredibly steep talus slope. At the top, find the rock you threw from the viewpoint across the void.

At **19.7** miles, you're back on the bike again. Crest a high point at **20.4** miles and coast to a fork—turn left on Pot Peak Trail 1266 toward Ramona trailhead. Put on your aviator goggles and get ready for takeoff; the next ten miles gets my vote as best singletrack descent ever. The first half mile is somewhat rough, but the trail soon smooths out and bliss follows. Descend the ridge between the North Fork and the main fork of Twenty-Five Mile Creek, across an open hillside. As the trail slaloms around Pot Peak, there are a few minor climbs and a short noodle or two, but the trail soon cruises into deeper woods, continuing the sharp descent. Finally, at **30.1** miles, reach Ramona Campground to complete this truly epic loop.

Gazetteer

Nearby camping: Ramona Park Campground (USFS, primitive), Twenty-Five Mile Creek State Park, Lake Chelan State Park
Nearest food, drink, services: Chelan

30 CHELAN
Twenty-Five Mile Creek
✿✿✿✿

Distance	25.5 miles
Ride	Loop; singletrack, dirt road; views
Duration	5 to 8 hours
Travel time	Wenatchee—1 hour; Seattle—4 hours
Hill factor	Long, strenuous dirt-road climb; 4,780-foot gain
Skill level	Intermediate
Season	Late summer, fall
Maps	Green Trails: Brief; USFS: Entiat Ranger District
Users	Bicyclists, equestrians, hikers, motorcyclists
More info	Wenatchee National Forest, Chelan District, 509-682-2576

Prelude

This long ride gains an impressive chunk of elevation, but it doesn't quite epic-qualify because the climb is entirely on a dirt road, and there isn't any hike-a-biking or complicated route-finding. Still, it's a tough ride. Of course, the descent is so fun—a veritable Jedi run—that you will surely forget the strenuous climb before completing the loop. Remember to pop your ears on the descent. When I rode this loop, snow covered the last few miles of Forest Road 5900, making the climb an interesting challenge. To eliminate some of the climbing and distance, you may want to shuttle partway up the road.

To Get There

From Wenatchee, travel north on Alternate US Highway 97 up the west side of the Columbia River. Past the town of Entiat, turn left on State Route 971 (Navarre Coulee Road) toward Lake Chelan State Park. After about 7 miles, turn left on South Lakeshore Drive and proceed north along Lake Chelan. Pass Twenty-Five Mile Creek State Park on your right. Soon after, turn left onto Shady Pass Road (Forest Road 5900) and set your odometer to zero. At 2.8 miles, the road forks: Turn left and drop down FR 8410, which is gravel. At 3.2 miles, reach tiny Ramona Campground on the right. Park here.

The Ride

From Ramona Campground, ride back up FR 8410 toward Shady Pass Road. The climbing begins immediately. At **0.5** mile, reach a fork and take a hard left on FR 5900, which is dirt. The road climbs west, then begins the long series of switchbacks up the wide ridge toward Grouse Mountain. At **1.5** miles, bypass Twenty-Five Mile Creek Trail on the left. Pass FR 5903 on the left at **2.6** miles. Continue up the main road, avoiding lesser spurs while catching occasional views of Lake Chelan. At **6.2** miles, 2,600 feet above the starting point, pass by Grouse Mountain Campground on the right. (Parking is available at this campground, if you are considering a shuttle.)

From the campground, FR 5900 climbs steadily up the high ridge between Lake Chelan and the Twenty-Five Mile Creek drainage. At **8.6** miles, pass a viewpoint and continue climbing. After a couple of miles, the road levels, then descends to Chesapeake Saddle, **11.2** miles. From the saddle, the road heads up again at a steep grade toward Crescent Hill. At

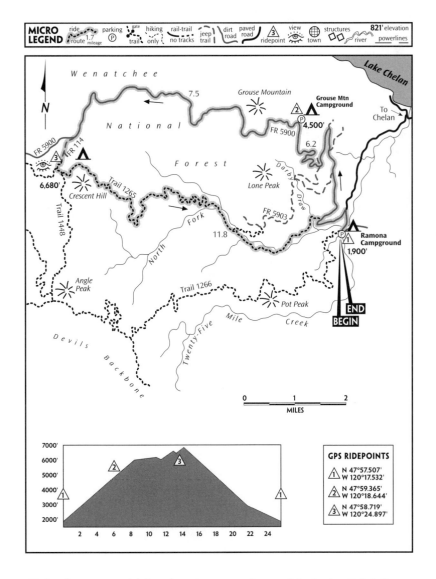

12.8 miles, cross a high point, then pass the road to Junior Point Campground on the left. When the road forks after a short descent, bear left on FR 114 toward Devils Backbone trailhead. Stay to the right (don't drop to Handy Spring Campground); the road ends at the trailhead, **13.7** miles. The high, flat area near the trailhead affords great views of Glacier Peak Wilderness to the northwest and the Sawtooth Mountains to the northeast.

Wide and loose, Devils Backbone Trail 1448 climbs steeply from the end of the road, probably mandating a hike. Reach a fork at **13.9** miles, and bear left. When the trail forks again at **14** miles, turn left onto Twenty-Five Mile Creek Trail 1265. True singletrack begins here. The trail climbs for a quarter mile, then noodles over dome-topped Crescent Hill. At **14.5** miles, begin the sweet, singletrack descent. Keep your speed moderate. A few stretches of the trail are rocky and technical; others are steep and capped with cement pavers, which provide great traction but can be quite disconcerting if you aren't expecting them.

At **18.1** miles, enter a deeper forest. A few miles farther, the trail runs along North Fork of Twenty-Five Mile Creek. At **21.5** miles, reach a fork: Turn right, continuing down Trail 1265. This is easy to miss. **WHOA!** At **22.8** miles, watch out for the vertical runway down a steep set of pavers. At **24** miles, the trail ends at FR 5900—turn right and descend. At **25** miles, just as you reach pavement, take a hard right turn onto FR 8410. Drop to Ramona Campground at **25.5** miles to complete the loop.

Gazetteer

Nearby camping: Ramona Park Campground (USFS, primitive), Twenty-Five Mile Creek State Park, Lake Chelan State Park
Nearest food, drink, services: Chelan

31 CHELAN
Darby Draw
✹✹✹

Distance	10.4 miles
Ride	Loop; singletrack, dirt road
Duration	2 to 3 hours
Travel time	Wenatchee—1 hour; Seattle—4 hours
Hill factor	Moderately difficult climb, steep in parts; 1,700-foot gain
Skill level	Intermediate
Season	Summer, fall
Maps	Green Trails: Brief; USFS: Entiat Ranger District
Users	Bicyclists, equestrians, hikers, motorcyclists
More info	Wenatchee National Forest, Chelan District, 509-682-2576

Road 5903 with Lake Chelan in the background

Prelude

Not interested in a 4,000-foot climb like you'll find on the nearby Pot Peak Epic (Ride 29) or Twenty-Five Mile Creek (Ride 30)? Well, here's the short version of Twenty-Five Mile Creek—half as long and with a third of the climbing. But this loop still comes with a few lofty views of Lake Chelan and some rocking singletrack. Similar to its longer, more challenging cousins, Darby Draw begins with a dirt-road climb and ends with a fast singletrack descent.

To Get There

From Wenatchee, travel north on Alternate US Highway 97 up the west side of the Columbia River. Past the town of Entiat, turn left on State Route 971 (Navarre Coulee Road) toward Lake Chelan State Park. After about 7 miles, turn left on South Lakeshore Drive and proceed north along Lake Chelan. Pass Twenty-Five Mile Creek State Park on your right. Soon after, turn left onto Shady Pass Road (Forest Road 5900) and set your odometer to zero. At 2.8 miles, the road forks: Turn left and drop down FR 8410, which is gravel. At 3.2 miles, reach tiny Ramona Campground on the right. Park here.

The Ride

From Ramona Campground, ride back up FR 8410 toward Shady Pass Road. At **0.5** mile, reach a fork and take a hard left on FR 5900 (Shady Pass Road is to the right). The road climbs west toward Darby Draw, then switchbacks to the east, quickly gaining altitude. At **1.5** miles, pass Twenty-Five Mile Creek Trail on the left. When you reach a fork at **2.6** miles, turn left onto FR 5903. The road climbs at a healthy rate, then descends into Darby Draw. Across the creek, begin climbing again around the low southern edge of Lone Peak. At **5.1** miles, reach a fork in the road and go left on FR 100 toward Lone Peak trailhead.

At **5.6** miles, reach Lone Peak trailhead. Take the singletrack, Trail 1264, toward North Fork Twenty-Five Mile Creek. At **6.8** miles, after a steep descent, arrive at Twenty-Five Mile Creek Trail 1265. Turn left and descend toward the creek. WHOA! At **8** miles, watch out for an unexpected, extremely steep descent down a carpet of cement pavers—disconcerting, to say the least. Keep your speed down because you may prefer to walk this short section. At **8.9** miles, the trail ends at FR 5900—turn right and descend the gravel road. At **9.9** miles, just as you reach

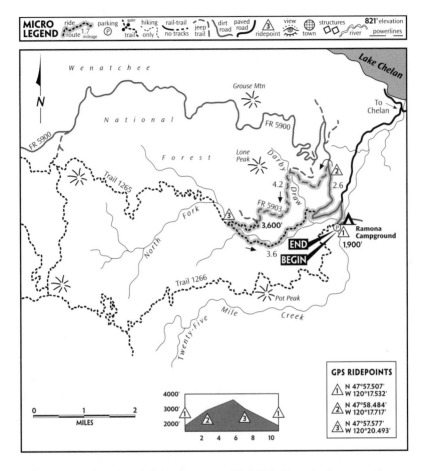

pavement, take a hard right turn onto FR 8410. Drop to Ramona Campground at **10.4** miles to complete the loop.

Gazetteer

Nearby camping: Ramona Park Campground (USFS, primitive), Twenty-Five Mile Creek State Park, Lake Chelan State Park
Nearest food, drink, services: Chelan

32 Echo Ridge

◐◐

Distance	8 miles
Ride	Loop; doubletrack, dirt road, singletrack; views
Duration	1 to 2 hours
Travel time	Wenatchee—1 hour; Seattle—4 hours
Hill factor	Rolling terrain, gentle climbs, ascents; 460-foot gain
Skill level	Beginner
Season	Summer, fall
Maps	USFS: Echo Ridge Trails
Users	Bicyclists, equestrians, hikers
More info	Wenatchee National Forest, Chelan District, 509-682-2576

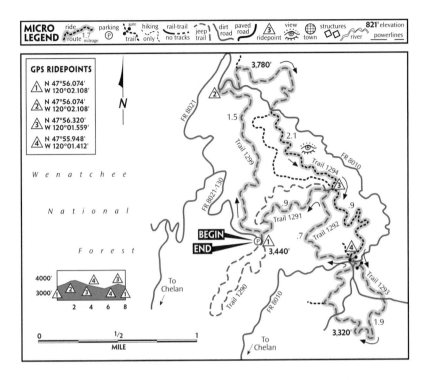

Prelude

The trail system at Echo Ridge delivers gentle grades on primarily double-track trails, across open, grassy hillsides scattered with the occasional pine. Since the tree cover is limited, you may want to plan your ride on either side of the day's heat in July and August. The ridgeline affords grand views of Lake Chelan to the southwest and the Okanogan to the northeast. Lots of trails crisscross the area, and you're never too far from the trailhead, so it's perfect for families and beginning mountain bikers. Ride carefully here; equestrians, walkers, and runners also use these trails.

To Get There

From the intersection of Sanders Street and Woodin Avenue in the town of Chelan, turn east on Sanders Street toward State Route 150, and set your odometer to zero. Go one block and turn left on Johnston Avenue (SR 150). At 2.2 miles, turn right on Boyd Road. At 4.9 miles, take the left fork, following the signs toward Echo Ridge. At 5.7 miles, take the right fork up Cooper Gulch. At 6.8 miles, turn right on Cooper Gulch Road. As the road becomes dirt at 9.6 miles, pass Echo Valley Ski Area. At 9.8 miles, take the right fork toward Echo Ridge. At 11.1 miles, take the right fork. At 12.1 miles, take the left fork. Reach the Echo Ridge trailhead parking area at 12.2 miles.

The Ride

From the trailhead, go to the left of the kiosk and take No Where to Hide Trail 1299, a grassy and somewhat rough doubletrack. The trail wraps around the open, sagebrushy hillside, ascending at a moderate rate. At **1.5** miles, reach a dirt road and turn right. At **1.7** miles, turn left on Little Critter Trail 1295, a doubletrack. At **1.8** miles, ignore a trail on the left—stay on the ragged doubletrack. Crest a high point, then gradually descend to a T at a dirt road, **2.7** miles. Turn left on the road, then immediately stop: The road continues left and two trails fork off to the right. Take the middle route, Morning Glory Trail 1294. After a short climb, this trail winds and dances down the broad, open ridge.

At **3.6** miles, reach a five-way intersection known as Grand Junction. Bear left on Zippidy-Do-Da Trail 1292 and continue cruising the ridge-line. At **4.5** miles, reach a four-way intersection (Chaos Corner) and bear left toward Trail 1293. A few pedal strokes farther, reach a dirt road: Turn left, then immediately right on Alley Opp Trail 1293. At **4.9** miles, cross a dirt road and continue up Trail 1293. This doubletrack drops to a low point at the **5.3**-mile mark. At **5.7** miles, cross a dirt road, again continuing on Trail 1293. A few tire rotations farther, the trail divides: Go right (the trail to the left leads to a viewpoint).

At **6.3** mile, follow the trail across two dirt roads. After the second, bear to the left, returning to the four-way, Chaos Corner intersection. From here, turn left on Wind Singer Trail 1292. At **7.1** miles, arrive back at Grand Junction and turn left on Chickadee Trail 1291, an old dirt road. Almost immediately the trail forks—bear left, staying on Chickadee Trail. This trail drops quickly, heading west. When the old road forks at **7.8** miles, bear left and continue descending. At **8** miles, reach the trailhead to complete the loop.

Gazetteer

Nearby camping: Ramona Park Campground (USFS, primitive), Twenty-Five Mile Creek State Park, Lake Chelan State Park
Nearest food, drink, services: Chelan

33 Cutthroat Lake

✸✸✸

Distance	4 miles
Ride	Out & Back; singletrack; views
Duration	1 hour
Travel time	Wenatchee—2.5 hours; Bellingham—3.5 hours; Seattle—4.5 hours
Hill factor	Gradual climb to lake; 480-foot gain
Skill level	Intermediate
Season	Late summer, fall
Maps	Green Trails: Washington Pass
Users	Bicyclists, equestrians, hikers
More info	Okanogan National Forest, Methow Valley District (Winthrop), 509-996-4000

Trail 483

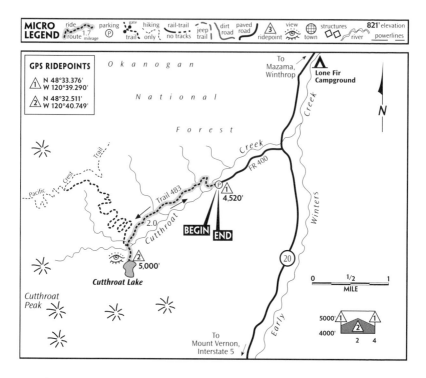

Prelude

Before you ride the trail to Cutthroat Lake, you must repeat this mantra 500 times: "I promise not to ride fast, I promise not to ride fast." Surrounded by high, jagged peaks and talus slopes, this beautiful mountain lake makes an excellent destination. The trail to the lake is short and easy, so it's heavily traveled by families. Do not ride fast. If you're interested in a harder climb, a longer route, or a faster descent, there are plenty of other rides in the Methow Valley. Take this one at a slow pace and enjoy the scenic beauty.

To Get There

From Interstate 5 just north of Mount Vernon, take State Route 20 east. After about 100 miles, cross Washington Pass. About 4 miles east of the pass, turn left on Forest Road 400. Drive up FR 400 for 1 mile and reach the trailhead parking for Cutthroat Lake Trail. (Alternate Route: From the town of Winthrop, drive west on SR 20. After 27 miles, turn right onto FR 400.)

The Ride

The trail to Cutthroat Lake begins at the parking area, immediately crosses over Cutthroat Creek, and ascends easily. Occasional roots and rocks pose a technical challenge, but the wide, hard-packed trail is forgiving. The trail climbs at an even grade toward the Cutthroat Lake basin, which is surrounded by 7,000-foot peaks. The granite-gray trail, the small scattered pines, and the ring of peaks to the southwest provide a stark beauty. When the trail divides at **1.8** miles, turn left (the right fork climbs at an incredibly steep rate toward Cutthroat Pass, where it meets the Pacific Crest Trail). Walk across the creek, then follow the meandering trail to Cutthroat Lake, **2** miles. After soaking up the views and eating a snack, turn around and pedal slowly back to the trailhead to complete the ride, **4** miles.

Gazetteer

Nearby camping: Lone Fir Campground (USFS), Klipchuck Campground (USFS)
Nearest food, drink, services: Mazama

METHOW VALLEY
34 Cedar Creek

⊕⊕⊕⊕

Distance	12.4 miles
Ride	Out & Back; singletrack
Duration	2 to 4 hours
Travel time	Wenatchee—2.5 hours; Bellingham—3.5 hours; Seattle—4.5 hours
Hill factor	Tough, technical singletrack climb; 1,860-foot gain
Skill level	Expert
Season	Summer, fall
Maps	Green Trails: Washington Pass, Mazama
Users	Bicyclists, equestrians, hikers
More info	Okanogan National Forest, Methow Valley District (Winthrop), 509-996-4000

Cedar Falls

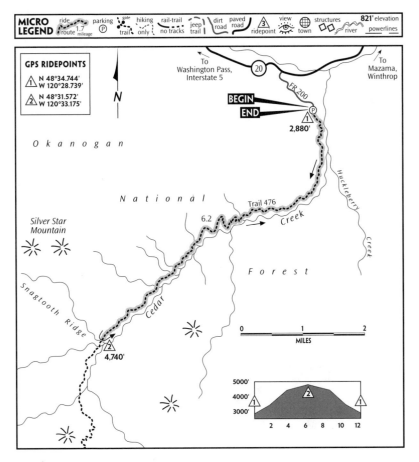

Prelude

The first section of this trail to Cedar Creek Falls is heavily used, so watch for other trail users. Beyond the falls, the trail becomes very technical, with rocks, gnarls of roots, and a narrow tread all mandating expert riding skills. For skilled riders, though, the trail along Cedar Creek provides a good skill test; the long, deep valley offers a scenic setting. As I bounced down the jarring descent, I readily admit that I coveted the plush ride of a full-suspension bike.

To Get There

From Interstate 5 just north of Mount Vernon, take State Route 20 east. After about 100 miles, cross Washington Pass. About 13 miles east of the pass, turn right on Forest Road 200. Drive up FR 200 for 0.9 mile and reach the large dirt trailhead parking for Cedar Creek Trail 476. (Alternate Route: From the town of Winthrop, drive west on SR 20. After 17.5 miles, turn left onto FR 200.)

The Ride

From the trailhead, ride out Cedar Creek Trail 476. The trail, at times rocky and technical, climbs at a moderate rate. As the trail swings to the west, pass Cedar Falls on the left at **1.8** miles. From here, the ascent is steeper and the trail becomes much more difficult to ride. For less skilled riders, the way is a hike-a-bike from this point out as it ascends the deep valley between North Gardner Mountain to the south and Silver Star Mountain to the north. The way levels somewhat at the **3.5**-mile mark. Stay on the main trail as it parallels Cedar Creek. At **6.2** miles, reach an unnamed Cedar Creek tributary that originates in the high crags of Snag-tooth Ridge. From here, the trail gets more difficult and steeper; some riders may want to continue, but for this ride, turn around here and ride back to the trailhead, **12.4** miles.

Gazetteer

Nearby camping: Lone Fir Campground (USFS), Klipchuck Campground (USFS)
Nearest food, drink, services: Mazama

35 Rader Creek

✿✿✿

Distance	13.2 miles
Ride	Loop; singletrack, doubletrack, dirt road
Duration	2 to 3 hours
Travel time	Wenatchee—2 hours; Bellingham—4 hours; Seattle—5 hours
Hill factor	Moderately steep climbs; 1,280-foot gain
Skill level	Intermediate
Season	Summer, fall
Maps	Green Trails: Buttermilk Butte, Twisp; MVSTA: Sun Mountain Trails
Users	Bicyclists, equestrians, hikers
More info	Okanogan National Forest, Methow Valley District (Winthrop), 509-996-4000; Methow Valley Sports Trails Association, 509-996-3287

Prelude

Sun Mountain and the Methow Valley Sports Trails Association (MVSTA) do a great job of signing and maintaining the Sun Mountain trail system. A trail fee program may be instituted in the future to keep the trails in good shape for summer recreation. That's okay because it's a fun place to ride, none of the rides are too difficult, and it's tough to get lost here, despite the hodgepodge of dirt roads, doubletracks, and singletracks. For an excellent

Patterson Lake

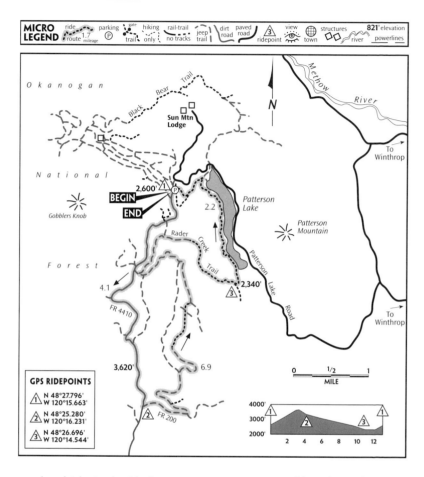

weekend trip to the Methow, you may want to combine the Rader Creek loop with one of the longer, more strenuous Methow Valley rides.

To Get There

From the town of Winthrop, drive south on State Route 20. Just after crossing the Methow River, about 0.25 mile south of town, reach a fork and bear right on Twin Lakes Road toward Sun Mountain Lodge. Start your odometer here. At 3.3 miles, reach a fork and go right on Patterson Lake Road, following the signs for Sun Mountain. Pass Patterson Lake on the left. At 8.8 miles, take the left fork on Thompson Ridge Road (Forest Road 4410) to Chickadee trailhead. Almost immediately, turn left again into the trailhead parking area.

The Ride

From Chickadee trailhead, ride out to Thompson Ridge Road and turn left. The dirt road climbs around the southwest side of Gobblers Knob toward Thompson Ridge. During the moderately difficult ascent, pass numerous trails and lesser roads on both sides of the main road. Climb up the main road to the top at **3.2** miles. From here, the road rolls down to a fork at **4.1** miles. Take a hard left onto Meadow Lark Trail (aka FR 200). **WHOA!** Don't get going to fast, or you will miss this turn. Descend on this ragged dirt road to a fork at **4.9** miles and turn left, continuing on Meadow Lark. The road drops a short distance, crosses Thompson Creek, then begins climbing. Pass Goshawk Trail on the right at **5.4** miles. The road levels, then cuts a fast traverse to a barbed-wire fence. Leave the fence the way you found it, open or closed.

When the road forks at **5.9** miles, bear right on Blue Jay Trail, which is a doubletrack. Blue Jay twists and winds, becoming singletrack for a while. At a four-way intersection of trails, **7.4** miles, ride straight through, continuing on Blue Jay. Almost immediately, reach a T and turn left onto the doubletrack. At **8** miles, Blue Jay ends at a T—turn right onto Meadow Lark, a jeep track at this point. The rough jeep track traverses, then descends sharply down a rocky tread. At **8.8** miles, reach a fork and bear right on Lower Inside Passage. Just across Rader Creek, **8.9** miles, turn right again, continuing down Lower Inside Passage. The rough and rock-jumbled doubletrack descends, following Rader Creek.

At **9.5** miles, reach a fork and turn right on Rader Creek Trail. The doubletrack soon becomes a winding singletrack. Pass through two gates on this fast descent. Reach a fork at **11** miles and turn left on Patterson Lake Trail. After a short meander, the trail traverses the western shore of Patterson Lake. Climb away from the lake, then, at **12.5** miles, reach a T and turn left on Cabin Trail. After another short ascent, the trail forks at **13** miles—bear right on Chickadee. At **13.2** miles, return to Chickadee trailhead to complete the loop.

Gazetteer

Nearby camping: Black Pine Lake Campground (USFS), Beaver Creek Campground (Washington State Department of Wildlife, primitive)
Nearest food, drink, services: Winthrop

36 Yellow Jacket Trail

Distance	2.6 miles
Ride	Loop; wide singletrack, dirt road
Duration	1 hour
Travel time	Wenatchee—2 hours; Bellingham—4 hours; Seattle—5 hours
Hill factor	Easy, rolling trail; 80-foot gain
Skill level	Beginner
Season	Summer, fall
Maps	Green Trails: Buttermilk Butte; MVSTA: Sun Mountain Trails
Users	Bicyclists, equestrians, hikers
More info	Okanogan National Forest, Methow Valley District (Winthrop), 509-996-4000; Methow Valley Sports Trails Association, 509-996-3287

Hough Homestead

Prelude

The Yellow Jacket ride is a short, easy afternoon ditty for the family. There are no difficult climbs or challenging trails here, just a nice jaunt to the Hough Homestead and back. As with all the trails in the Sun Mountain system, good trail signs make it simple to get around.

To Get There

From the town of Winthrop, drive south on State Route 20. Just after crossing the Methow River, about 0.25 mile south of town, reach a fork and bear right on Twin Lakes Road toward Sun Mountain Lodge. Start your odometer here. At 3.3 miles, reach a fork and go right on Patterson

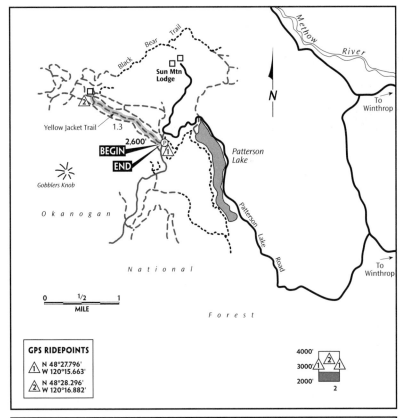

Lake Road, following the signs for Sun Mountain. Pass Patterson Lake on the left. At 8.8 miles, take the left fork on Thompson Ridge Road (Forest Road 4410) to Chickadee trailhead. Almost immediately, turn left again into the trailhead parking area.

The Ride

From Chickadee trailhead, ride back to Thompson Ridge Road. Cross the dirt road to Rodeo trailhead. Bear left onto Rodeo, a wide trail on which you can roll easily. At **0.2** mile, take the right fork. At **0.4** mile, bear left at the fork. When the trail forks at **0.7** mile, bear left on Rodeo. At **1.2** miles, reach a road at the Hough Homestead and turn left toward Yellow Jacket. The road climbs, but just before the gate, **1.4** miles, take Yellow Jacket Trail on the left. The trail rises and falls, heading southeast below Gobblers Knob. At a fork, **2.4** miles, stay to the left. After a short distance, cross Thompson Ridge Road and follow the signs to the parking lot and Chickadee trailhead. Reach the parking area at **2.6** miles to complete the loop.

Gazetteer

Nearby camping: Black Pine Lake Campground (USFS), Beaver Creek Campground (Washington State Department of Wildlife, primitive)
Nearest food, drink, services: Winthrop

METHOW VALLEY
37 Black Bear Trail
☼☼☼

Distance	9.1 miles
Ride	Loop; singletrack, doubletrack, dirt road
Duration	1 to 3 hours
Travel time	Wenatchee—2 hours; Bellingham—4 hours; Seattle—5 hours
Hill factor	Easy to moderate climbing; 480-foot gain
Skill level	Intermediate
Season	Summer, fall
Maps	Green Trails: Buttermilk Butte, Twisp; MVSTA: Sun Mountain Trails
Users	Bicyclists, equestrians, hikers
More info	Okanogan National Forest, Methow Valley District (Winthrop), 509-996-4000; Methow Valley Sports Trails Association, 509-996-3287

Storm gathering in the Methow Valley

Prelude

With a nice mix of dirt roads and singletrack, short climbs and twisting descents, the Black Bear loop offers a fun ride without the exhaustion that comes with some of the other Methow Valley rides. There are way too many intersections, forks, and turns on this ride, but all the trails at Sun Mountain are well signed, making the route-finding easy. I rode this loop on a blustery October afternoon that threatened the first snow of the season, and I was grateful for the well-signed trails that minimized my standing-around-staring-at-the-map time.

To Get There

From the town of Winthrop, drive south on State Route 20. Just after crossing the Methow River, about 0.25 mile south of town, reach a fork and bear right on Twin Lakes Road toward Sun Mountain Lodge. Start your odometer here. At 3.3 miles, reach a fork and go right on Patterson Lake Road, following the signs for Sun Mountain. Pass Patterson Lake on the left. At 8.8 miles, take the left fork on Thompson Ridge Road (Forest Road 4410) to Chickadee trailhead. Almost immediately, turn left again into the trailhead parking area.

The Ride

From Chickadee trailhead, ride back to Thompson Ridge Road. Cross the dirt road to the trailhead, then bear right onto Beaver Pond Trail. When the wide trail forks at **0.4** mile, bear left, remaining on Beaver Pond Trail. At **1.5** miles, reach Hough Homestead: Bear left, cross over a stream, and then take an immediate right onto Fox Loop. At **1.8** miles, reach a fork and go left toward Aqua Loop. After passing through a cattle gate, reach another fork and turn right. At **2** miles, reach a road and bear right, continuing toward Aqua Loop. At **2.4** miles, turn right and drop down to the aqueduct to begin the loop. When the trail forks at **2.8** miles, bear left. At **3.1** miles, reach a road and go left. When the road forks a few pedal strokes farther, stay to the right. Bear to the right again at **3.2** miles.

At **3.7** miles, a trail exits the road on the left. Take this trail toward Fox Loop. At **3.9** miles, reach a T and turn left, riding back through the cattle gate toward Fox. Just up the trail, reach another fork and go left on Fox. From here, the narrow dirt road descends. At **4.3** miles, reach a fork and turn left on Black Bear Trail. At **4.6** miles, the road ends and a singletrack

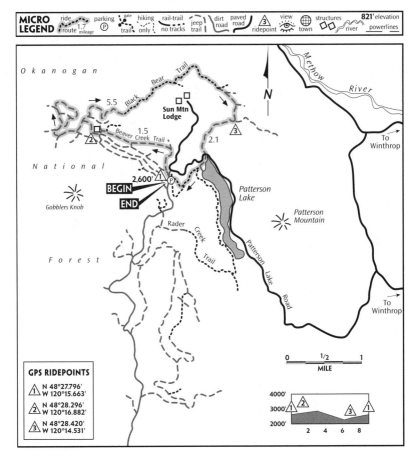

Okanogan

Black Bear Trail

5.5

Sun Mtn Lodge

Beaver Creek Trail 1.5

2.1

National

2,600'

BEGIN

END

Gobblers Knob

Patterson Lake

Rader Creek Trail

Forest

Patterson Mountain

Patterson Lake Road

To Winthrop

To Winthrop

Methow River

N

0   1/2   1
MILE

GPS RIDEPOINTS

1 N 48°27.796'
   W 120°15.663'

2 N 48°28.296'
   W 120°16.882'

3 N 48°28.420'
   W 120°14.531'

4000'
3000'
2000'

2 4 6 8

begins in its place. After a short rise, the trail begins a downward traverse above Wolf Creek. After a fun, winding descent, ride into an open area that affords grand views of the lower Methow Valley. Pass through a cattle gate at **5.7** miles. After a short, steep climb, reach a fork and bear left. Ride back into the woods and continue climbing.

At around the **6.3**-mile mark, the trail levels, then passes through another cattle gate. After a sweet little descent, reach a fork, bear right on the dirt road, and begin climbing. One pedal rotation farther, the road forks—go right toward Patterson Lake. Reach another fork at **7.2** miles and go right toward Sun Mountain. The dirt road reaches the paved Patterson Lake Road at **7.8** miles. Cross the paved road to a trail on the opposite side and bear right. Keep the Patterson Lake Cabins on

your left, following the trail around to the lake. At **8.1** miles, bear right on Patterson Lake Trail. At **8.4** miles, reach a fork and go right on Cabin Trail. After another short ascent, the trail forks at **8.8** miles—bear right on Chickadee. At **9.1** miles, arrive at Chickadee trailhead to complete the loop.

Gazetteer

Nearby camping: Black Pine Lake Campground (USFS), Beaver Creek Campground (Washington State Department of Wildlife, primitive)
Nearest food, drink, services: Winthrop

38 Starvation Mountain

✺✺✺✺

Distance	31.2 miles
Ride	Loop; singletrack, doubletrack, dirt road; views
Duration	4 to 8 hours
Travel time	Wenatchee—2 hours; Bellingham—4 hours; Seattle—5 hours
Hill factor	Long, strenuous dirt-road climb; 4,360-foot gain
Skill level	Intermediate
Season	Late summer, fall
Maps	Green Trails: Twisp, Loup Loup, Tiffany Mountain, Doe Mountain
Users	Bicyclists, equestrians, hikers
More info	Okanogan National Forest, Methow Valley District (Twisp), 509-997-2131

The future: an eleven-mile singletrack descent

Prelude

In spite of the epic length and elevation gain, this route is ridable the entire way, thus the four-wheel rating. Still, it's a long and difficult four-wheeler, so pack extra food, water, and clothes in preparation for this big ride. The dirt-road climb is relentless, so being in good condition doesn't hurt either. The descent, arguably the best in the Methow Valley, will keep you smiling. Also, the weather at the 7,000-foot summit can be vastly different from conditions at the start. When I rode this loop in early October, it was sunny and warm at Beaver Campground, snowing when I topped out near Starvation Mountain, and hot again as I traversed the steep, exposed slopes high above Beaver Creek.

To Get There

Set your odometer to zero in the town of Twisp and travel east on State Route 20. At 2 miles, turn left, continuing on SR 20 toward Okanogan. At about 4.8 miles, turn left on Beaver Creek Road (County Road 1637). At 10.3 miles, reach primitive Beaver Campground on the right. Park here.

The Ride

From the campground, ride northwest up Upper Beaver Creek Road (now Forest Road 4225). The road forks at **0.5** mile—bear right on FR 4225 toward Loup Loup Summit. The road, which follows South Fork of Beaver Creek, climbs steadily. Pass Trail 406 on the left, then at **3.5** miles, pass Bear Mountain Trail 442 on the right. When the road forks at **4.6** miles, turn left onto FR 4230. From the fork, the road heads up quickly, grabbing big chunks of elevation. At **5.7** miles, crest a high point and descend. At **6.9** miles, pass Trail 406 on the left.

When the road forks at **7.5** miles, take the lesser road, FR 190, on the right. Rough and rutted, FR 190 climbs in fits and starts. At **7.9** miles, ignore a road on the right; continue up FR 190. Reach a T at **8.8** miles and turn left onto FR 4235. Descend for a short stretch, then bypass FR 100 on the right, **9.3** miles. Just beyond, ignore several lesser spurs—continue up the main road, climbing now. At **10.4** miles, pass FR 200 and Lightning Creek Trail 425 on the left. Continue up the main road, which climbs relentlessly. Pass Shrew Creek Trail on the right as you mount Beaver Ridge toward Starvation Mountain. At **15.3** miles, about one-quarter mile short of the summit, find an unmarked jeep trail on the left. Check out the outstanding views of the surrounding Okanogan

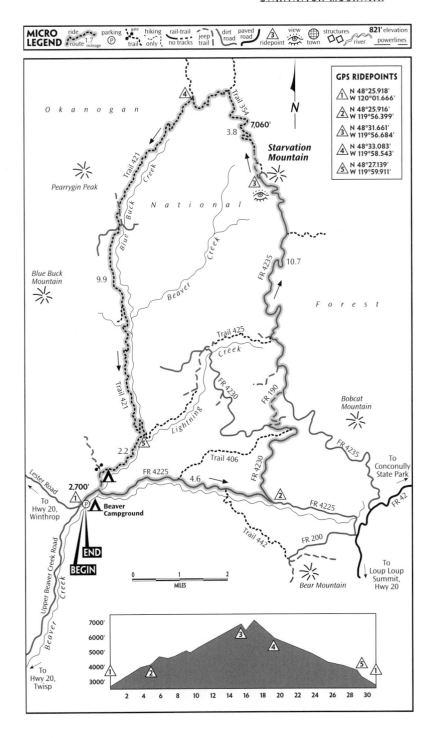

MICRO LEGEND — ride route 1.7 mileage | parking Ⓟ | gate trail | hiking only | rail-trail no tracks | jeep trail | dirt road | paved road | ridepoint | view town | structures river | 821' elevation powerlines

GPS RIDEPOINTS

⚊1 N 48°25.918' W 120°01.666'
⚊2 N 48°25.916' W 119°56.399'
⚊3 N 48°31.661' W 119°56.684'
⚊4 N 48°33.083' W 119°58.543'
⚊5 N 48°27.139' W 119°59.911'

Okanogan

Pearrygin Peak

Trail 421

Blue Buck Creek

National

Blue Buck Mountain

9.9

Trail 421

Beaver Creek

Trail 354

3.8

7,060'

Starvation Mountain

⚊3

FR 4235

10.7

Forest

Trail 425

Creek

FR 4230

FR 190

Bobcat Mountain

Lightning

Creek

⚊5

2.2

FR 4225

Trail 406

4.6

FR 4230

⚊2

FR 4235

To Conconully State Park

FR 42

Lester Road

2,700'

⚊1

Ⓟ Beaver Campground

To Hwy 20, Winthrop

FR 4225

Trail 442

FR 200

To Loup Loup Summit, Hwy 20

Bear Mountain

Upper Beaver Creek Road

Beaver Creek

To Hwy 20, Twisp

END

BEGIN

0   1   2
MILES

7000'
6000'
5000'
4000'
3000'

⚊1 ⚊2 ⚊3 ⚊4 ⚊5 ⚊1

2 4 6 8 10 12 14 16 18 20 22 24 26 28 30

National Forest. After an energy bar and a rack of Fig Newtons, turn left on the unmarked jeep trail, cross a berm, and head down.

After a short descent, the well-used unmarked jeep trail joins the little-used official trail: Bear left onto Trail 354 and pass through a wood gate. The wide trail drops to a saddle, **15.8** miles, then switchbacks to the north up Blue Buck Ridge. Though quite steep, this ascent is potentially ridable for those with fresh legs; however with 4,100 feet already climbed, it's probably a push for most. By the time you gain the crest of Blue Buck Ridge, **16.8** miles, you'll have spent every calorie consumed a mile and a half earlier. From the top, the trail roars down the north-facing slope toward Beaver Meadow. Stay on the main trail to a fork at **19.1** miles, then take a hard left turn onto Blue Buck Trail 421 and continue the blistering descent on a smooth trail.

WHOA! The next section is somewhat confusing. At **22.7** miles, reach an old dirt road and turn left. At **22.9** miles, bear to the right and regain the trail, which parallels the old road. At **23.2** miles, cross the road and continue down Blue Buck Trail 421. From here, the singletrack takes off again, zipping down along Blue Buck Creek. When the trail forks at **25.4** miles, stay to the left. As the trail begins a long traverse, edging upward, ride from a pine and fir forest to a dry, open hillside, far above Beaver Creek. The trail, loose and less stable than before, angles across the high western side of the ravine, in and out of the contours. At around the **28.3**-mile point, drop down several switchbacks and cross Beaver Creek. Reach a T at **29** miles and turn right onto Lightning Creek Trail. At **30.2** miles, enter a primitive camp; the trail widens to become a doubletrack. At **30.3** miles, reach FR 200, turn left, and descend. Arrive at the junction of FR 200 and FR 4225, **30.7** miles. Turn right onto FR 4225 and pedal back to Beaver Campground to compass the loop, **31.2** miles.

Gazetteer

Nearby camping: Beaver Creek Campground (Washington State Department of Wildlife, primitive), Loup Loup Campground (USFS)
Nearest food, drink, services: Twisp

39

METHOW VALLEY

Lightning Creek

☼☼☼

Distance	17.4 miles
Ride	Loop; singletrack, dirt road
Duration	2 to 4 hours
Travel time	Wenatchee—2 hours; Bellingham—4 hours; Seattle—5 hours
Hill factor	Tough dirt-road climb; 2,620-foot gain
Skill level	Intermediate
Season	Summer, fall
Maps	Green Trails: Twisp, Loup Loup
Users	Bicyclists, equestrians, hikers
More info	Okanogan National Forest, Methow Valley District (Twisp), 509-997-2131

Prelude

Lightning Creek is one of the more popular Methow Valley rides. It's a stout (some sections of the dirt-road climb are unexpectedly steep) but very

Forest Road 4235 toward Lightning Creek and Starvation Mountain

intermediate ride—not too long and without too much elevation gain, but lots of fun. In fact, once you reach the top of the ride, pedaling is optional. Lightning, it seems, refers not only to the weather in the area but also the speed-of-light descent; just don't zap any other trail users on the way down. I combined this ride with Bear Mountain (Ride 40) for a longer day.

To Get There

Set your odometer to zero in the town of Twisp and travel east on State Route 20. At 2 miles, turn left, continuing on SR 20 toward Okanogan. At about 4.8 miles, turn left on Beaver Creek Road (County Road 1637). At 10.3 miles, reach primitive Beaver Campground on the right. Park here.

The Ride

From the campground, ride northwest on Upper Beaver Creek Road (now Forest Road 4225). The road forks at **0.5** mile—bear right on FR 4225 toward Loup Loup Summit. The road, which follows South Fork of Beaver Creek, climbs steadily. Pass Trail 406 on the left, then, at **3.5** miles, pass Bear Mountain Trail 442 on the right. When the road forks at **4.6** miles, turn left onto FR 4230. From the fork, the road climbs quickly. At **5.7** miles, crest a high point and descend. At **6.9** miles, pass Trail 406 on the left. When the road forks at **7.5** miles, take the lesser road, FR 190, on the right. Rough and rutted, FR 190 climbs in fits and starts. At **7.9** miles, ignore a road on the right; continue up FR 190. Reach a T at **8.8** miles and turn left onto FR 4235. Descend for a short stretch, then bypass FR 100 on the right, **9.3** miles. Just beyond, ignore several lesser spurs—continue up the main road, climbing.

At **10.4** miles, just as FR 200 exits on the left, take a hard left and ride down Lightning Creek Trail 425, which originates between FR 4235 and FR 200. This is the end of mandatory pedaling. The trail drops to Lightning Creek, bends to the right, and zips down along the creek. After a fun singletrack descent, the trail becomes an old road (FR 100). At **12.3** miles, reach a T and turn right on FR 4230. After a few pedal strokes, turn left onto another old road (FR 125), following the signs for Lightning Creek Trail 425, and continue the descent. The old road peters into a singletrack around the **13.1**-mile mark. From here, the trail traverses down the north side of Lightning Creek. Occasional stretches of technical riding, a steep side slope, and the scenic valley below are the only things that keep you honest during this fast descent.

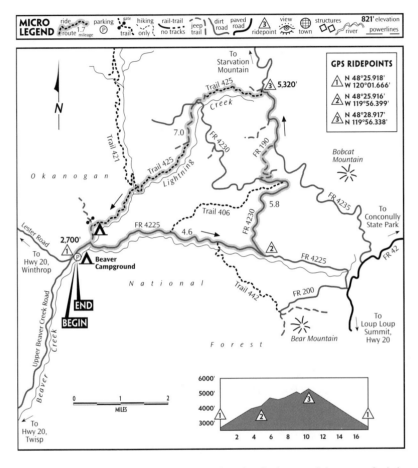

At **15** miles, ride through the creek twice before arriving at a fork in the trail. Bear left, continuing down Trail 425. The descent is more modest now, but still fun. Cross a cattle guard at **16.2** miles, and ride into a dispersed camp area. At **16.3** miles, reach FR 200 and turn left. When the road forks at **16.9** miles, bear right onto Upper Beaver Creek Road (FR 4225). Arrive back at Beaver Creek Campground at **17.4** miles to complete the loop.

Gazetteer

Nearby camping: Beaver Creek Campground (Washington State Department of Wildlife, primitive), Loup Loup Campground (USFS)
Nearest food, drink, services: Twisp

40

METHOW VALLEY
Bear Mountain

☼☼☼

Distance	14.7 miles
Ride	Loop; singletrack, dirt road
Duration	2 to 4 hours
Travel time	Wenatchee—2 hours; Bellingham—4 hours; Seattle—5 hours
Hill factor	Moderately difficult dirt-road climb; 2,320-foot gain
Skill level	Advanced
Season	Summer, fall
Maps	Green Trails: Twisp, Loup Loup
Users	Bicyclists, equestrians, hikers
More info	Okanogan National Forest, Methow Valley District (Twisp), 509-997-2131

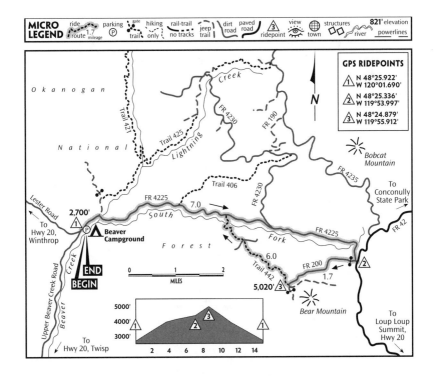

Prelude

The Bear Mountain trail can function as a healthy trip for some riders or an extra loop for the very fit (see Option, below). After climbing a series of dirt roads toward Loup Loup Summit, the trail, recently constructed with mountain bikers in mind, weaves down the north side of Bear Mountain. Parts of the descent are fast and smooth, but some sections have not yet been compacted and are somewhat rough.

To Get There

Set your odometer to zero in the town of Twisp and travel east on State Route 20. At 2 miles, turn left, continuing on SR 20 toward Okanogan. At about 4.8 miles, turn left on Beaver Creek Road (County Road 1637). At 10.3 miles, reach primitive Beaver Campground on the right. Park here.

The Ride

From the campground, ride northwest on Upper Beaver Creek Road (now Forest Road 4225). The road forks at **0.5** mile—bear right on FR

4225 toward Loup Loup Summit. The road, which follows South Fork of Beaver Creek, climbs steadily. Pass Trail 406 on the left. At **3.5** miles, pass Bear Mountain Trail 442 on the right. When the road forks at **4.6** miles, stay to the right on FR 4225. From here, the road climbs more gently as it eases toward South Fork Meadows. At **6.1** miles, ignore a spur road on the right that cuts across the meadow. After crossing over South Fork of Beaver Creek at **6.6** miles, follow the main road as it heads south. At **7** miles, reach a four-way intersection: Just before FR 4225 touches FR 42 (paved), turn right onto FR 200. Ride around the gate, ignore FR 202 (a cross-country ski trail) on the right, and begin the tough climb up the north flank of Bear Mountain.

At the **8.6**-mile mark, just before FR 200 switchbacks up to the left, turn right on Bear Mountain Trail 442. (**WHOA!** Don't ride through the gate on FR 220.) The trail drops down from the road, following a fence line. At **8.9** miles, pass through a gate: Leave the gate as you found it. From the gate, the trail rounds a knoll on the right, descending steadily. In places, the trail is rocky and rough, but for the most part the descent is fast and fun. Cross a dirt road at **10.3** miles, continuing down the trail toward South Fork of Beaver Creek. After a few steep switchbacks, cross the creek and climb a short distance to FR 4225, **11.2** miles. Turn left and ride back down to Beaver Campground to complete the loop, **14.7** miles.

Option

Ambitious riders may want to combine this loop with either Lightning Creek (Ride 39) or Starvation Mountain (Ride 38). From Bear Mountain's 11.2-mile mark, turn right and ride up FR 4225 to its junction with FR 4230 (the 4.6-mile point for both other rides). This option adds 7.7 miles to those rides.

Gazetteer

Nearby camping: Beaver Creek Campground (Washington State Department of Wildlife, primitive), Loup Loup Campground (USFS)
Nearest food, drink, services: Twisp

41

METHOD VALLEY
Pipestone Canyon

◉◉

Distance	11.8 miles
Ride	Loop; doubletrack, dirt road
Duration	1 to 3 hours
Travel time	Wenatchee—2 hours; Bellingham—4 hours; Seattle—5 hours
Hill factor	Moderately difficult dirt-road climb; 1,140-foot gain
Skill level	Beginner
Season	Summer, fall
Maps	Green Trails: Twisp
Users	Bicyclists, equestrians, hikers
More info	Okanogan National Forest, Methow Valley District (Twisp), 509-997-2131

Dropping in to Pipestone Canyon on a snowy day

Prelude

One of the Methow Valley's best-known mountain-bike rides, the typical Pipestone experience boils down to this: a short but strenuous dirt-road climb followed by a beautiful trip through the rocky canyon. The moderately tough climb and several tricky sections of trail through the canyon make this a more difficult two-wheeler, but it shouldn't demoralize anyone. The trip traverses land managed by numerous agencies, as well as some private holdings, so tread carefully. I rode this after a mid-October storm. The doubletracks were filled with puddles and the cold, heavy mist soaked me. I haven't been that cold since. Afterward, I went to the Duck Brand in Winthrop and gorged.

To Get There

Set your odometer to zero in the town of Twisp and travel east on State Route 20. At 2 miles, turn left, continuing on SR 20 toward Okanogan. At about 4.8 miles, turn left on Beaver Creek Road (County Road 1637). At 10.3 miles, reach the junction of Beaver Creek Road and Lester Road. Park near this junction.

The Ride

Begin this ride from the junction of Upper Beaver Creek Road (County Road 1637) and Lester Road (CR 1624), which is immediately south of Beaver Campground. From the junction, ride west up Lester Road toward Campbell Lake. Right from the start the climb is steep, as you ride up open, sagebrushy slopes dotted by a few pines. Stay on the main road, passing several lesser spurs. At **1.5** miles, the road levels and traverses. Campbell Lake sits in the basin below on the left. Achieve the high point at **2.2** miles, then coast down the road into the Campbell Lake basin. WHOA! Watch for cars on the road.

When Lester Road meets Campbell Lake Road, **3.5** miles, turn left and pedal easily along Campbell Lake Road. Ride by the lake at **4.4** miles. After passing through a fence, **4.8** miles, the road becomes a narrow, at times brushy doubletrack, as it drops into Pipestone Canyon. The ride through the canyon is fast, but be sure to take a break and check out the angular rock formations. At **6.2** miles, pass through another fence. At **7.6** miles, reach an awkward four-way intersection: Take a shallow left, remaining on the main road. The road follows a fence line above a field. When you reach Balky Hill Road at **8.4** miles, turn left. At **8.9** miles, Balky

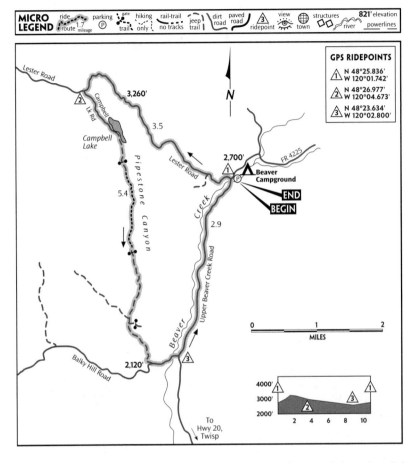

Hill Road ends at a T with Upper Beaver Creek Road—turn left and pedal up the road. Climb steadily on Upper Beaver Creek Road to its junction with Lester Road to complete the loop, **11.8** miles.

Gazetteer

Nearby camping: Beaver Creek Campground (Washington State Department of Wildlife, primitive), Loup Loup Campground (USFS)
Nearest food, drink, services: Twisp

42

METHOW VALLEY

Twisp River Trail

○○○

Distance	15.9 miles
Ride	Loop; singletrack, paved road
Duration	2 to 4 hours
Travel time	Wenatchee—2 hours; Bellingham—4 hours; Seattle—5 hours
Hill factor	Gradual paved-road climb; 880-foot gain
Skill level	Advanced
Season	Summer, fall
Maps	Green Trails: Buttermilk Butte, Stehekin
Users	Bicyclists, equestrians, hikers
More info	Okanogan National Forest, Methow Valley District (Twisp), 509-997-2131

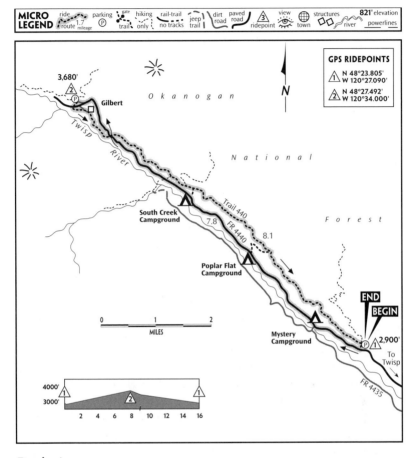

Prelude

This route climbs up a gently graded paved road and then heads down a rocky singletrack to form a narrow loop. Watch for vehicles on the paved forest road as you climb. On the trail, especially on wet days, gnarls of roots and large, loose rocks make the upper section very challenging, and I don't recommend it for beginners. For skilled riders, though, the twisty, jarring descent makes for a fun ride. Several inches of snow covered the ground when I traversed this trail. It was beautiful, but the snow, combined with the technical tread, made the first several miles a wet hike-a-bike.

To Get There

From the town of Twisp, turn west on Twisp River Road (County Road 9114) and set your odometer to zero. Stay on Twisp River Road, which after about 14 miles is also known as Forest Road 44. At 18.1 miles, turn right onto FR 220, toward Slate Creek trailhead. At 18.2 miles, reach the trailhead, and park.

The Ride

Ride down the hill back to FR 44 and turn right. The paved road climbs gently up the Twisp River valley. Pass Mystery Campground on the left at **0.9** mile and then Poplar Flat Campground on the left at **3** miles. At **5.2** miles, ride by South Creek trailhead, also on the left. At **7.7** miles, turn right on FR 457 toward the Twisp River trailhead. Almost immediately, the road ends. Several trails originate from this trailhead: Take Twisp River Trail 440 to the left.

The rocky trail descends away from the parking area and then crosses a road. At **8.1** miles, reach a T, turn right onto an old dirt road, and pass through the tiny ghost town of Gilbert. Cross North Creek and continue down the rough trail. At **8.9** miles, cross FR 44 and continue down the trail. Rocky and root covered, the trail rises and falls, making it difficult to get a rhythm. The first few miles of trail may be a hike-a-bike for less skilled riders. At **10.3** miles, pass a trail on the right that heads toward South Creek Camp. At **10.8** miles, ignore Scatter Creek Trail on the left. At **10.9** miles, reach a fork and turn left, continuing on Twisp River Trail 440. WHOA! This turn is not so intuitive. After a climb, the trail smooths out and traverses the steep slope above Twisp River. At **12.9** miles, reach a fork and bear left, traversing. Cross a series of talus slopes around the **13.6**-mile mark. Afterward, the trail zips down to a fork at **15.7** miles: Bear right toward the trailhead. Reach the trailhead at **15.9** miles to finish the ride.

Gazetteer

Nearby camping: Black Pine Lake Campground (USFS), Poplar Flat Campground (USFS), Mystery Campground (USFS, primitive)
Nearest food, drink, services: Twisp

43 METHOW VALLEY
Eagle Lakes
✿✿✿✿

Distance	13 miles
Ride	Out & Back; singletrack; views
Duration	3 to 4 hours
Travel time	Wenatchee—2 hours; Bellingham—4 hours; Seattle—5 hours
Hill factor	Strenuous singletrack climb; 2,340-foot gain
Skill level	Advanced
Season	Late summer, fall
Maps	Green Trails: Prince Creek; USFS: Twisp Ranger District
Users	Bicyclists, equestrians, hikers, motorcyclists
More info	Okanogan National Forest, Methow Valley District (Twisp), 509-997-2131

Prelude

After a ride up to Eagle Lakes, every mountain biker should appreciate the motorized users on this trail and others in the Sawtooth backcountry.

Middle Eagle Lake, frozen in mid October

Each year a nearby motorcycle club helps maintain these trails, clearing blowdown. In addition, the motorcycles help keep the tread compact and smooth, making bicycle riding easier and hike-a-biking less frequent. Of course the real treat of this ride isn't the compact trail, it's that we can ride our bikes up to a place as stunningly beautiful as Eagle Lakes.

To Get There

From the town of Twisp, drive east on State Route 20. After about 2 miles, bear right on SR 153 and head south toward Carlton, Methow, and Pateros. About 3 miles south of Carlton, turn right onto Gold Creek Loop Road. After a little more than a mile, turn right on Gold Creek Road toward Foggy Dew Campground. Zero out your odometer here. At 1 mile, bear right, continuing toward Foggy Dew. Afterward, Gold Creek Road is also known as Forest Road 4340. At 5.3 miles, pass FR 200 and Foggy Dew Campground on the left. From here, the road is dirt. At 6.9 miles, turn left on FR 300 toward Crater Creek. Continue up the steep main road. At 11.6 miles, reach the parking area for Eagle Lakes Trail.

The Ride

From the parking area, take Eagle Lakes Trail 431. With nary a place for a spin of the pedals for warm-up, the trail starts the strenuous climb toward Sawtooth Ridge. Reach a fork in the trail at **0.7** mile, and bear right. Ride over the bridge that spans Crater Creek and reach another fork: Bear left, riding up Trail 431. When the trail forks again at **1** mile, stay to the right. From here, the compact, nicely graded trail grinds up the ridge through a fir and, sporadically, larch forest, heading west. Shift into your low gear, tape your hands to the climbing bars, and go. At **2.4** miles, the trail forks—bear right, continuing the grueling climb toward Eagle Lakes.

As you ascend toward the lakes and Horsehead Pass beyond, the forest opens up and the views are remarkable. On hot summer days, though, the scattered forest and south-facing slope make this ride a scorcher. At around the **4.5**-mile mark, the trail becomes rocky and the riding more difficult. As you round a high point at **5.8** miles, Mount Bigelow comes into view. Drop down a rough trail into the Eagle Lakes basin. At **5.9** miles, reach a fork and bear right. The trail passes Middle Eagle Lake, then climbs toward Mount Bigelow. Attain Upper Eagle Lake at **6.5** miles. After you've used up all your film and dunked in the lake, turn around and return to the trailhead to complete the ride, **13** miles.

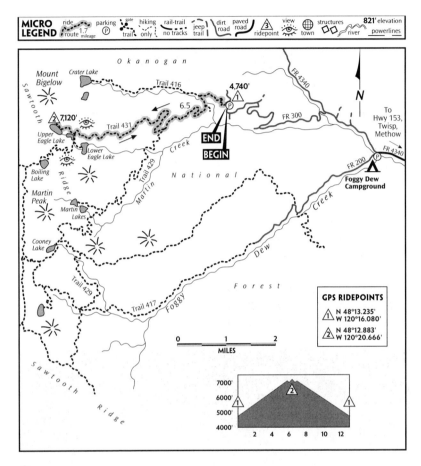

Option

There are a number of options—all rigorous—for riders determined to go farther. From the fork at 5.9 miles, go left. The trail forks again about one-quarter mile after crossing the creek. The left fork leads to Lower Eagle Lake, about one mile below. The right forks heads up to Horsehead Pass, about three-quarters of a mile above. From there, many difficult but stunningly beautiful trails explore the Sawtooth Mountains. Get the Green Trails Prince Creek map, and be sure to allow lots of time.

Gazetteer

Nearby camping: Foggy Dew Campground (USFS)
Nearest food, drink, services: Methow

44

METHOW VALLEY
Foggy Dew Epic
✻✻✻✻✻

Distance	26.8 miles
Ride	Loop; singletrack, dirt road; views
Duration	5 to 8 hours
Travel time	Wenatchee—2 hours; Bellingham—4 hours; Seattle—5 hours
Hill factor	Extreme, some hike-a-bike; 5,140-foot gain
Skill level	Advanced
Season	Late summer, fall
Maps	Green Trails: Prince Creek; USFS: Twisp Ranger District
Users	Bicyclists, equestrians, hikers, motorcyclists
More info	Okanogan National Forest, Methow Valley District (Twisp), 509-997-2131

Following another mountain biker who misjudged the seasons

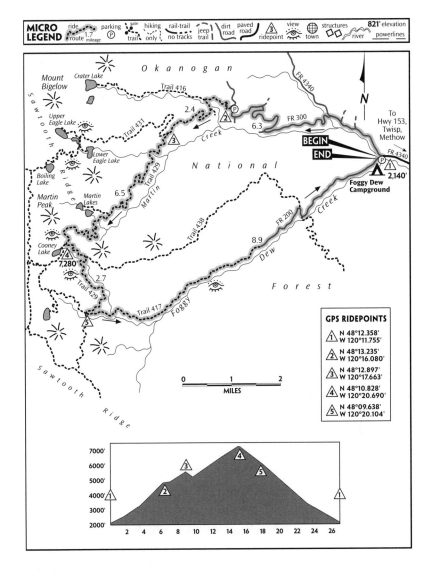

Prelude

Start early, bring lots of food and water, and don't rush the first six miles. When I compassed this route on a crisp day in mid-October, the lower, south-facing slopes up Forest Road 300 were warm, but as I singletracked past Martin Lakes, patches of snow covered the trail. In the register log at the trailhead, I noticed that another rider had ridden this same loop just the day before, so I felt confident that the first snow of the season had melted sufficiently to clean the loop. But on the steep slopes up toward Cooney Lake, patches of snow soon became a continuous snowpack. It was a push from here to the top, as it had been the day before, and I followed the tracks of my adventurous predecessor—two feet and a wheel track through the snow. By the time I attained the saddle near Cooney Lakes, the sun had gone over the ridge. I changed shirts, put on my warm clothes and a hat, and hike-a-biked down the snowy slopes toward Foggy Dew Creek, following the snowy tracks. Luckily, I soon descended below the snow line, and the trail down Foggy Dew proved smooth and fast, a truly great descent. I reached the road before dark. But the real truth to this ride isn't the epic descent or elevation gain, and it isn't the nicely graded singletrack, either. The truth is the overwhelming, rugged beauty of the Sawtooth Range, the stunning peaks, high lakes, and yellow October larch against blue sky. Adventure, beauty, and a good story came together here.

To Get There

From the town of Twisp, drive east on State Route 20. After about 2 miles, bear right on SR 153 and head south toward Carlton, Methow, and Pateros. About 3 miles south of Carlton, turn right onto Gold Creek Loop Road. After a little more than a mile, turn right on Gold Creek Road toward Foggy Dew Campground. Zero out your odometer here. At 1 mile, bear right, continuing toward Foggy Dew Campground. From here, Gold Creek Road is also known as Forest Road 4340. At 5.3 miles, turn left on FR 200. At 5.4 miles, find Foggy Dew Campground on the left. Park here.

The Ride

From the junction of FR 4340 and FR 200, begin by riding up FR 4340, which is dirt from this point on. The road aims north, climbing above the eastern bank of Gold Creek at a healthy grade. Bypass several lesser spurs on the right. At **1.6** miles, reach a fork and turn left on FR 300. From here, head west and ride along Crater Creek. The climb is steeper here, but manageable. At **3.6** miles, the road cuts a hairpin turn to the right, away from the creek, and begins mounting Raven Ridge. For the next mile, the road is ridiculously steep, and hookeybobbing—grabbing on to your friend's bike for a tow—may be the only option. After burning a dozen doughnuts' worth of calories, reach a fork and bear right, continuing up the main road. Just beyond, the grade subsides to plain hard.

After **6.3** miles and 2,600 feet of climbing, reach Eagle Lakes trailhead on the left. (You may want to shuttle a car to this point.) Take Trail 431, and begin the strenuous singletrack climb toward the Cooney Lakes basin. Reach a fork in the trail at **7** miles, and bear right. Ride over the bridge that spans Crater Creek and reach another fork: Bear left, continuing up Eagle Lakes Trail 431. When the trail forks again at **7.3** miles, stay to the right. From here, the compact, nicely graded trail grinds up the ridge through a fir forest, heading west up the sharp ridge between Crater Creek and Martin Creek. When the trail forks at **8.7** miles, bear left on Martin Creek Trail 429. Zip down a number of quick switchbacks, a nice break in the climbing. At **9.7** miles, cross the creek and start ascending again. Traverse up the forested valley toward Martin Peak; the climb is relentless. At **13** miles, the trail forks—bear left, continuing toward Cooney Lakes.

After the fork, the trail crosses a creek, then switchbacks up the south base of Martin Peak. The grade remains similar (grueling), but the trail becomes narrow, rocky, and generally more challenging as the climb progresses. Beyond the **14**-mile mark, the forest opens up and more views of Sawtooth Ridge are evident. At **15.1** miles, achieve the saddle that separates the Martin Creek valley and the Foggy Dew Creek valley. From here, the trail drops to a fork at **15.2** miles. Go left, descending Trail 429 toward Foggy Dew (the right fork heads up to Cooney Lake). Next: a 3,600-foot singletrack descent. Steep and rocky, the trail descends into a maze of high ridges. Pass the faint Foggy Dew Ridge Trail on the left. Drop down to cross a creek, and ride in to a deeper forest. Watch out for other trail users.

The trail bends west for a short time, then reaches a T at **17.9** miles. Turn left onto Foggy Dew Trail 417 and continue the sharp descent, heading east now. The trail, smooth and fast, follows Foggy Dew Creek. Pass Foggy Dew Falls on the right at **20.2** miles. At **23.1** miles, the trail ends at the Foggy Dew trailhead parking area. From here, ride down the main road, FR 200, descending toward Foggy Dew Campground. Pass the campground and reach FR 4340 at **26.8** miles to complete the loop.

Gazetteer

Nearby camping: Foggy Dew Campground (USFS)
Nearest food, drink, services: Methow

45

Wallace Falls

☉☉☉

Distance	19 miles
Ride	Out & Back; singletrack, dirt road, rail-trail; views
Duration	3 to 5 hours
Travel time	Seattle—1 hour; Bellingham—2 hours
Hill factor	Moderately difficult climb; 1,540-foot gain
Skill level	Intermediate
Season	Late spring, summer, fall
Maps	USGS: Wallace Lake, Gold Bar
Users	Bicyclists, hikers
More info	Washington State Parks, 800-233-0321

Wallace Falls

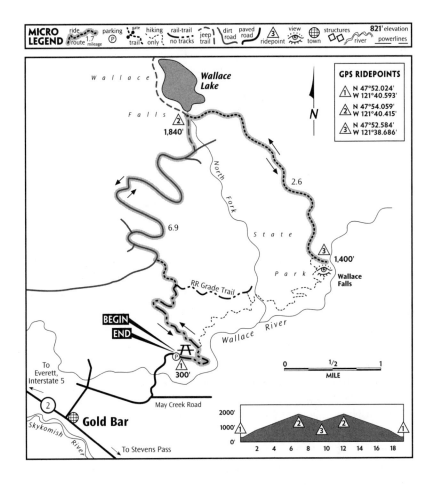

Prelude

For the first several miles, you'll ride up an old logging railroad grade—a rail-trail—through a verdant forest. Beyond the rail-trail, the route slogs up a dirt road toward Wallace Lake, affording occasional views of the Skykomish River valley. The long climb to the lake, combined with the rough, rocky trail to the falls, makes this a difficult three-wheel ride. Though Wallace Falls is spectacular, skipping the falls and just riding to the lake for a picnic is a fine outing.

To Get There

From Everett, take US Highway 2 east toward Stevens Pass. After about 28 miles, reach the small town of Gold Bar. From Gold Bar, turn left onto First Street and then right onto May Creek Road. When the road forks, take the left fork, following the signs to Wallace Falls State Park. Park here.

The Ride

From the parking lot, ride along the wide gravel trail under the power lines. At **0.3** mile, the trail bends left into the woods. Pass the Woody Trail on the right, **0.4** mile. The trail, an old logging railroad grade, climbs steadily away from the Wallace River. At **1.6** miles, reach a fork at a kiosk: Turn left and ride up a steep, narrow trail. As the trail hairpins to the right at **1.8** miles, ignore the trail on the left. The trail ends at a dirt road. Turn right onto the road and continue ascending toward Wallace Lake. Stay on the main road as it switchbacks upward. Pass by a road on the right, **4.1** miles. Reach another fork at **4.4** miles, and go right, staying on the main road. Arrive at yet another fork at **6.3** miles—turn left onto the darker, narrower jeep trail that climbs toward Wallace Lake.

When you reach Wallace Lake at **6.9** miles, the wide trail ends at a T— turn right and cross the short bridge, following the signs to Wallace Falls (the trail to the left travels to the opposite end of the lake). Just past the bridge, stay on the main trail to the right. The way descends, at times rocky, rough, and wet. At **7.8** miles, pass through a very wet section, with large puddles and water running across the trail. After a gradual climb, pass by a lesser trail on the left. WHOA! At **9.5** miles, pass a sign: "Walk Zone." And walking is a good idea, unless you want to plunge off the cliff and become part of Wallace Falls. From the Walk Zone, a hiking-only trail accesses a number of spectacular views of the falls. When you are done exploring, turn around and retrace your pedal strokes back to the Wallace Falls State Park trailhead, **19** miles, to complete the loop.

Gazetteer

Nearby camping: Money Creek Campground (USFS)
Nearest food, drink, services: Gold Bar

46

SAUK RIVER
Monte Cristo Townsite
◉◉

Distance	8 miles
Ride	Out & Back; gated dirt road
Duration	1 to 2 hours
Travel time	Seattle—2 hours; Bellingham—2 hours
Hill factor	Gradual dirt-road climb; 420-foot gain
Skill level	Beginner
Season	Summer, fall
Maps	Green Trails: Sloan Peak, Monte Cristo
Users	Bicyclists, hikers
More info	Mount Baker-Snoqualmie National Forest, Darrington District, 360-436-1155

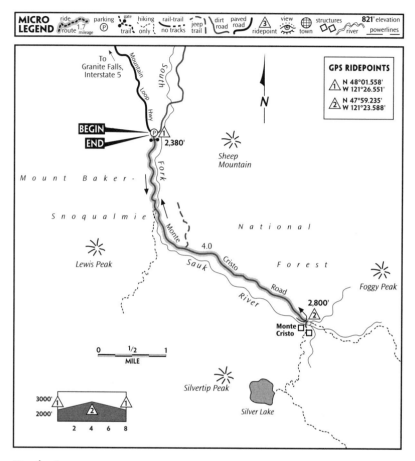

GPS RIDEPOINTS

| △1 | N 48°01.558' W 121°26.551' |
| △2 | N 47°59.235' W 121°23.588' |

Prelude

Heavily used in summer by hikers and bicyclists (keep your speed down and be friendly), the road to Monte Cristo climbs gently south from Barlow Pass along the South Fork of the Sauk River. The gated dirt road heads to a historic mining town clinging to life near the headwaters of the Sauk. A few residents still live in Monte Cristo, at least part of the year, working active mining claims. The residents keep the road somewhat maintained for their personal vehicles, so you may encounter one during the ride. At the end of the road, you can explore the small town or take advantage of one of the many bike-and-hike opportunities. From Monte Cristo, steep trails ascend to Silver Lake, Twin Lakes, and Glacier Basin, all wonderful destinations within Henry M. Jackson Wilderness.

To Get There

From Everett, take US Highway 2 east toward Stevens Pass. After about 5 miles, turn left on State Route 9. Drive about 5 miles farther and turn right on SR 92 toward Granite Falls. From Granite Falls, take the Mountain Loop Highway toward Verlot and Barlow Pass. About 19 miles from Granite Falls, reach the pass and turn left into a parking area.

The Ride

From the parking area at Barlow Pass, carefully cross the Mountain Loop Highway to the gated Monte Cristo Road. Ride up the road, following the South Fork of the Sauk River. Other than a few small ups and downs, the road stays level for the first mile. At **1** mile, cross the river at Twin Bridges Camp. You may want to walk across this cobbled-together bridge. Across the river, the road climbs gently as it bears to the southeast. Pass several spur roads on the right and left: Continue up the main road. The climb gradually becomes more difficult. The road bends to the right and reaches a bridge over the river, **4** miles. There's a bike rack just before the bridge. Leave your bike at the rack and carefully cross the river on foot. After exploring the Monte Cristo townsite, return to the bike rack and pedal back to Barlow Pass to complete the ride, **8** miles.

Gazetteer

Nearby camping: Perry Creek Campground (USFS, primitive), Bedal Campground (USFS, primitive)
Nearest food, drink, services: Verlot

SAUK RIVER

47 White Chuck Bench

☉☉☉

Distance	12.8 miles
Ride	Loop; singletrack, dirt road
Duration	2 to 4 hours
Travel time	Seattle—2 hours; Bellingham—2 hours
Hill Factor	Gradual climb, some walking on trail; 640-foot gain
Skill level	Advanced
Season	Late spring, summer, fall
Maps	Green Trails: Sloan Peak
Users	Bicyclists, hikers
More info	Mount Baker-Snoqualmie National Forest, Darrington District, 360-436-1155

White Chuck River

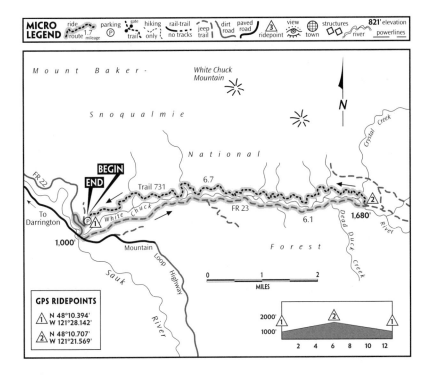

Prelude

This ride meanders up a dirt road along the White Chuck River, then returns to the parking area via a singletrack on the opposite side of the river. For the first few miles down White Chuck Bench Trail, roots, rocks, and a narrow tread conspire against all but the most skilled riders. Farther downriver, though, the trail widens and smooths out, and the riding becomes less technical. Even if you have to hike-a-bike some of the upper trail, this is a fine trip. Elephantine strands of moss hang from the low branches of late-succession cedar, ferns carpet the understory of the lush forest; meanwhile, the trail winds down to the river, speeds along it for a stretch, then climbs back up the river's northern bench.

To Get There

From Interstate 5 just north of Everett, take State Route 530 east toward the town of Darrington. After about 33 miles, reach Darrington, turn right onto the Mountain Loop Highway (Forest Road 20), and set your odometer to zero. At 9.4 miles, cross over the Sauk River, then immediately turn left on FR 22. The road crosses the White Chuck River, then bends to the left. At 9.6 miles, the road divides: Turn right. Climb up a road, past a gravel pit, to White Chuck Bench trailhead on the right at 9.8 miles. Park here.

The Ride

From the small gravel turnout at the White Chuck Bench trailhead, ride back down the road toward Mountain Loop Highway. Pass the gravel pit, then reach a T at **0.2** mile and turn left onto FR 22. The road crosses over the White Chuck River. At **0.3** mile, reach a T at Mountain Loop Highway (FR 20)—turn left. At **0.4** mile, turn left on FR 23 toward White Chuck trailhead. The road climbs gently along the White Chuck River. Stay on the main road, ignoring spurs. At **6.1** miles, FR 23 crosses over the White Chuck River. Just after crossing the river, turn left into a wide parking area for White Chuck Bench Trail 731. The trail begins, immediately narrow and winding, mossy and root-strewn. Using a series of one-log bridges, cross the numerous small streams that make up Crystal Creek. After a short climb, walk down a steep, very narrow trail into a draw. Carefully cross the creek, then hike up the opposite bank. At the top, **6.6** miles, reach a fork and turn left, following the WBT (White Bench Trail) signs.

The trail continues narrow, twisty, and rooty, weaving past gigantic cedar and old, mossy red alder along the north side of the White Chuck River. Quite technical, the trail sometimes zigzags along fern-lined forest trails, sometimes meanders along the river. At **8.4** miles, bear left onto a wider trail corridor, most likely an ancient road. At **9.2** miles, walk across a wide swath of rocks that mark an old flood. At **11.7** miles, cross Black Oak Creek on yet another log bridge. From here, the trail zips through a wet, mossy forest. Reach the trailhead at **12.8** miles to complete the loop.

Gazetteer

Nearby camping: Bedal Campground (USFS, primitive), White Chuck Campground (USFS, primitive)
Nearest food, drink, services: Darrington

48

BELLINGHAM
Squires Lake
☼☼☼

Distance	6.5 miles
Ride	Loop; singletrack, dirt road, jeep trail, paved road
Duration	1 to 2 hours
Travel time	Bellingham—30 minutes; Seattle—1.5 hours
Hill factor	Sharp climbs and descents; 720-foot gain
Skill level	Intermediate
Season	Spring, summer, fall
Maps	USGS: Lake Whatcom, Alger
Users	Bicyclists, equestrians, hikers
More info	Whatcom County Parks, 360-733-2900

Prelude

Both Whatcom and Skagit County Parks share ownership and management responsibilities for Squires Lake Park. According to Whatcom County Parks, Squires Lake Park itself is more of a walkers' refuge than a

Squires Lake

mountain-bike area, partly because there are so few trails and partly because it's an easy family hike. Be a considerate trail user! However, this loop is a bit of a kludge, combining an assortment of different types of roads and trails, only a few of which are actually inside Squires Lake Park. The result is a short but adventurous ride with lots of exploration potential.

To Get There

Take Interstate 5 northbound to exit 240, about 10 miles north of Mount Vernon. Set your odometer to zero at the end of the interstate ramp and turn right onto Lake Samish Road. At 0.7 mile, reach the stoplight in the tiny town of Alger. Turn left on Old Highway 99 (Nulle Road). At 2.6 miles, turn right into the Squires Lake Park trailhead parking area.

The Ride

From the trailhead, ride back toward Alger on Old Highway 99 (Nulle Road). It's easy to cruise this flat, paved stretch, but watch out for the traffic because cars drive fast on this piece of county road. At **1.9** miles, reach the four-way stop in Alger and turn left onto Alger–Cain Lake Road. At **2.1** miles, turn left onto a gated gravel road. The sign on the gate says "private" but also "hiking, horseback riding, and bicycling permitted." Ride in a kind manner so that this privilege isn't taken away. At **2.5** miles, reach a fork and turn left. Descend for a short distance, then begin a tough climb. At **2.8** miles, when the road divides, bear right and continue climbing. At **3.5** miles, reach a fork and go right. Crest the summit of the ride; check out the views of Lake Samish to the northwest and, on a clear day, the Olympic Mountains to the west.

Just beyond the summit, the road forks at **3.7** miles: Bear left (the road on the right climbs up to an even better viewpoint). Reach yet another fork at **3.9** miles and bear left. At **4** miles, take the right fork and climb. At **4.3** miles, take the left fork. Reach a T at **4.5** miles and turn right. The rocky road becomes a singletrack. **WHOA!** The trail meanders along the edge of a cliff, which is on the left. When the trail forks at **4.8** miles, bear left. At **5** miles, take the right fork and immediately reach a T—turn right again and ride up the old roadbed. You are now on the Squires Lake trail system. Remember: Lots of walkers use this area, so ride with care. Pass a trail on the right. The old road becomes a trail. At **5.3** miles, reach a fork and bear right. Arrive at a T at **5.5** miles and turn left on a wide trail. A

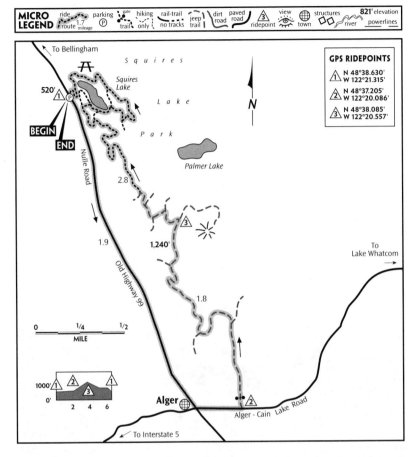

MICRO LEGEND · · · route ride 1.7 mileage · · · parking ℗ · · · gate · trail hiking · · · trail only rail-trail no tracks jeep trail dirt road paved road ⚠️3 ridepoint · · · view town structures river powerlines 821' elevation

To Bellingham

Squires Lake Park

Squires Lake

520' ⚠️1 ℗

BEGIN

END

Nulle Road

2.8

1.9

Old Highway 99

Palmer Lake

⚠️3

1,240'

1.8

GPS RIDEPOINTS

⚠️1 N 48°38.630' W 122°21.315'
⚠️2 N 48°37.205' W 122°20.086'
⚠️3 N 48°38.085' W 122°20.557'

N

To Lake Whatcom

0   1/4   1/2
MILE

1000' ⚠️1 ⚠️2 ⚠️3 ⚠️1
0'
2   4   6

Alger

Alger - Cain Lake Road

⚠️2

To Interstate 5

few pedal strokes farther, take the singletrack on the left. When the trail kisses the road at the **5.7**-mile mark, stay to the left.

When you reach a fork at **5.8** miles, go right. The trail glides along the edge of Squires Lake. Stay to the left as you round the lake on a wide gravel trail. At **6.2** miles, reach a fork and turn right. From here the trail switchbacks down to the parking area at the trailhead. Take it easy on this descent because lots of families use this trail to access the lake. Reach the trailhead at **6.5** miles to complete the loop.

Gazetteer

Nearby camping: Larrabee State Park
Nearest food, drink, services: Alger

49 BELLINGHAM
Blanchard Hill
⊕⊕⊕

Distance	10.6 miles
Ride	Out & Back; singletrack
Duration	2 to 3 hours
Travel time	Bellingham—20 minutes; Seattle—2 hours
Hill Factor	Difficult singletrack climb; 1,420-foot gain
Skill level	Intermediate
Season	Spring, summer, fall
Maps	USGS: Bellingham South, Bow; Happy Trails: Chuckanut Mountain
Users	Bicyclists, equestrians, hikers
More info	Washington State Department of Natural Resources, Northwest Region, 360-856-3500

Ascending Blanchard Hill toward Lily Lake and the Bat Caves

Prelude

Numerous trails circle and climb this lesser-known DNR property. This particular route, a singletrack up Mount Blanchard's south flank, switchbacks up toward several lakes as well as a high viewpoint that looks north toward Chuckanut Mountain. On the upper trail, the forest is thick and dark, the tread rough and root-strewn, so anytime after three in the afternoon a light might be a good idea. Also, where else can you explore the Bat Caves?

To Get There

Take Interstate 5 northbound to exit 240, about 10 miles north of Mount Vernon. Set your odometer to zero at the end of the interstate ramp and turn left. At 0.6 mile, take a hard left on Barrel Springs Road. At 1.3 miles, turn right onto B-1000, following the signs for Blanchard Hill Trail. At 1.9 miles, turn into a gravel parking area on the right.

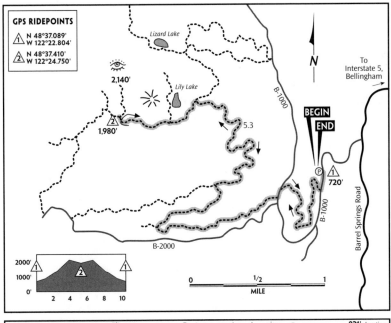

The Ride

From the parking area, ride down B-1000 away from Barrel Springs Road. After a few hundred yards, take the trail on the right that heads toward Lily Lake. The trail switchbacks up an open hillside, then traverses. At **1** mile, reach a dirt road (B-1000) and turn left. Almost immediately, find a trail on the right and take it. From here, the trail cuts a long traverse across the southern slope of Blanchard Hill, offering partial views of the Skagit River delta and the northern end of Whidbey Island. At **2.1** miles, as the trail switchbacks up the hill and ascends at a steeper rate, ignore a faint trail on the left. When you reach a fork at **2.5** miles, stay to the right and continue the easterly traverse in a dark forest.

From here the trail gets steeper and more technical, with lots of roots and rocks. At **3.9** miles, arrive at a T and turn left toward Lily Lake. The trail rolls and swells, but generally traverses through the wet forest. When the trail divides at **4.5** miles, bear left. At **5.3** miles, reach another fork. Stash your bike nearby and hike up the steep, gnarled right fork to the top of some steep cliffs. The views, and vertigo, are remarkable. From the top, hike back to the fork at **5.3** miles, then retrace your pedal strokes to the trailhead to complete the loop, **10.6** miles (plus one mile of hiking).

Option

From the fork at 5.3 miles, take the left fork. Descend for a short distance, then when the trail divides again, take the right fork and climb to the Bat Caves. I've included this optional addition because, while the views from the top of the cliffs are great, the allure of bat caves may be greater.

Gazetteer

Nearby camping: Larrabee State Park
Nearest food, drink, services: Alger, Bellingham

50 BELLINGHAM
Lookout Mountain

⚙⚙⚙⚙

Distance	12.9 miles
Ride	Loop; singletrack, dirt road, doubletrack; views
Duration	1 to 4 hours
Travel time	Bellingham—20 minutes; Seattle—2 hours
Hill factor	Constant up and down, steep; 1,040-foot gain
Skill level	Expert
Season	Spring, summer, fall
Maps	USGS: Bellingham South
Users	Bicyclists, equestrians, hikers
More info	Washington State Department of Natural Resources, Northwest Region, 360-856-3500

Prelude

To Bellingham mountain bikers, the vast area to the west and south of Lake Whatcom is known as Galbraith, although cartographers identify this rambling, sixteen-square-mile mountainous hump as Lookout Mountain. Whatever you choose to call it, the radical topography and nasty, twisted singletrack here have become synonymous with Bellingham mountain biking. The maze of trails, doubletracks, and dirt roads that wind frenetically over and across Galbraith's series of summits seem to purposely aim toward steep, log-strewn, root-packed, mossy, muddy, fern-laden stands of forest. Toss in panoramic views of Lake Samish, Bellingham, and the San Juans from the high points, and you begin to understand why one friend described the area as "Disneyland for idiots." Though the DNR manages a portion of the land on Lookout Mountain, much of the land is private property. The route described here—a conglomerate of trails and roads forming a figure eight—has been traversed by recreationalists for years, but that doesn't give us the right to use it, so ride with a Leave-No-Trace attitude. Of course, if "No Trespassing" signs are installed, you should respect them and look elsewhere to ride. Occasionally, parts of this area are signed "Closed" in the late summer as a precaution against forest fires—respect this too.

To Get There

Take Interstate 5 northbound to exit 246, about 15 miles north of Mount Vernon. Start your odometer at the end of the interstate ramp, then turn left on Samish Way toward Lake Padden. At 1.4 miles, turn left into the Upper Lake Padden trailhead parking area.

The Ride

From the Upper Lake Padden trailhead, turn right onto Samish Way. Almost immediately, turn left on Galbraith Lane. At **0.3** mile, the road divides: Bear left on North Galbraith Lane (don't turn right on Galbraith Lane). The road becomes gravel a short distance farther, then forks at **0.5** mile. Bear right, ride around the white gate, and begin climbing. When the road forks at **0.8** mile, stay to the right and continue up. Ignore a doubletrack back to the right at **0.9** mile. As the road eases toward a high point, pass several trails on the left (though not included in this route, they offer some excellent riding). Ride over the crest at **1.5** miles, then descend to a fork in the road at **1.9** miles. Take a hard right turn

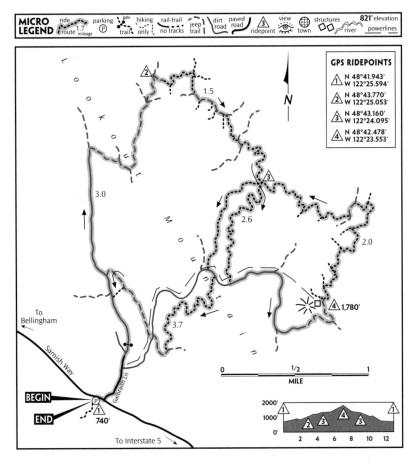

MICRO LEGEND: ride route, 1.7 mileage, parking (P), gate, hiking trail only, rail-trail no tracks, jeep trail, dirt road, paved road, 3 ridepoint, view, town, structures, 821' elevation, river, powerlines

GPS RIDEPOINTS

1. N 48°41.943' W 122°25.594'
2. N 48°43.770' W 122°25.053'
3. N 48°43.160' W 122°24.095'
4. N 48°42.478' W 122°23.553'

To Bellingham

Samish Way

Galbraith Ln

BEGIN

END 740'

To Interstate 5

and start climbing again. At a fork, **2.2** miles, bear right, staying on the main road. At **2.3** miles, take the left fork. Bypass trails on the right and left, then, at **2.8** miles, reach a three-pronged tridentlike fork: Take the middle route.

When the road forks at **3** miles, turn right onto the jeep trail that heads steeply upward, soon becoming a singletrack. The trail forks at **3.1** miles—go left. Pass a faint trail, then hit a T: Go right, ignoring a trail on the left and traversing across an open slope. When you reach a T at **3.3** miles, turn left and climb the steep, ragged jeep track. At **3.4** miles, reach a short flat spot and turn left (ignoring a trail on the right). After the turn, carefully count the trails on the right. At **3.6** miles, take the third singletrack on the right (note that the first and second form a nice little loop to a tree patch and back). After a few winding turns, the trail becomes a jeep track. At **3.9** miles, reach a T at a dirt road and turn right. WHOA! At **4** miles, take the first trail on the left, which is easily missed.

Much of the ride to this point can be thought of as strategic positioning. From here, the nasty twisties begin. The singletrack dives into the woods. After crossing a stream, follow the zigzagging trail through the dark, fern-drenched forest. At **4.5** miles, reach the four-way intersection; this is the center of the figure-eight route you are riding. Ride straight through the four-way along a narrow trail laced with gnarls of roots, tight corners, and short climbs. At **5.6** miles, the trail ends at a dirt road: Turn left and ride up the road, following a set of power lines. Stay on the main road, ascending at a moderate rate. When the road forks at **6** miles, bear right. After the fork, the road veers to the right and traverses the open hillside, affording views of Lake Samish to the southwest. At **6.5** miles, reach another fork and bear left. From here, the road is quite steep and the climb difficult. Ignore several lesser roads on the right. When the road forks at **6.9** miles, bear left and continue the steep climb. After a switchback, reach the summit at **7.1** miles.

After checking out the views, continue along the road, keeping the cell towers and communication equipment on your left. Almost immediately, the road ends and two trails head into the forest. Take the trail on the right. From here, take every right turn as you corkscrew and pinball down the most challenging section of this route. Endo potential: extreme. At the **7.8**-mile point, again turn right onto an ancient jeep track, and climb a short, steep hill. At **8** miles, reach a T and turn left (don't let déjà vu affect your judgment here). After a short climb, the trail ends at a T: Go left on the narrow dirt road. WHOA! After a short climb, take an easily missed singletrack on the right, beginning at **8.3** miles. Pass by two trails on the left, then finally drop into a small draw at **8.8** miles. Cross the creek and hike to the dirt road above. The road gradually descends to a fork at **9** miles—turn left. Shortly, the road becomes a singletrack and enters the woods.

At **9.1** miles, reach the four-way intersection at the center of the figure eight. Again, ride straight through the intersection. After a muddy slog down a wide trail, arrive at a T and turn left onto a dirt road, **9.8** miles. At **10** miles, reach another T and again turn left. Climb up the road for a short stretch, then take the faint singletrack on the right, which starts at **10.1** miles. The narrow, winding trail descends through tall brush. At **10.4** miles, reach a T and turn right, then quickly turn left onto a trail again. At **10.8** miles, reach another T; this time turn left, then quickly turn right onto a singletrack. When the trail ends at a double-track, **11.2** miles, bear right. At **11.4** miles, ride around a gate and reach a four-way intersection. Go straight, crossing the main road and riding along the ragged doubletrack. Ignore a trail on the left, cross a creek, and climb to a fork at **11.9** miles. Take a hard left turn onto a gravel road and begin descending. When the road forks, **12** miles, bear to the left. Ride around a white gate at **12.3** miles, and coast down North Galbraith Lane. Just after the road becomes paved, bear right. At **12.8** miles, carefully cross Samish Way to the Upper Padden Lake trailhead parking area to complete the loop at **12.9** miles.

Option

Sick of all the turn-here, turn-there route instructions? Use this book for the driving directions, then toss it and ride for many happy hours. One caveat: Bring your light and some warm clothes.

Gazetteer

Nearby camping: Larrabee State Park
Nearest food, drink, services: Bellingham

51 Lake Padden

✷

Distance	2.9 miles
Ride	Loop; trail
Duration	1 hour
Travel time	Bellingham—15 minutes; Seattle—2 hours
Hill factor	Nearly flat; 60-foot gain
Skill level	Beginner
Season	Year-round
Maps	North Cascades Institute: Bellingham Greenways; Happy Trails: Chuckanut Mountain
Users	Bicyclists, equestrians, hikers
More info	Bellingham Parks and Recreation, 360-676-6985

Lake Padden

Prelude

Wedged in a pocket between Chuckanut Mountain and Lookout Mountain, Lake Padden is located just south of Bellingham. The wide dirt trail around the lake has none of the dramatic topography of the neighboring mountains—it's a short, easy, beginner ride. Note that this trail is heavily used by walkers, runners, and equestrians. Remember to yield to all other users. Always stop and talk quietly to the horse and rider as they pass.

To Get There

Take Interstate 5 northbound to exit 246, about 15 miles north of Mount Vernon. Start your odometer at the end of the interstate ramp, then turn left on Samish Way toward Lake Padden. At 1.4 miles, pass the Upper Lake Padden trailhead parking area on the left. At 2.6 miles, pass the east entrance to Lake Padden Park on the left. At 3 miles, turn left into the west entrance of Lake Padden Park.

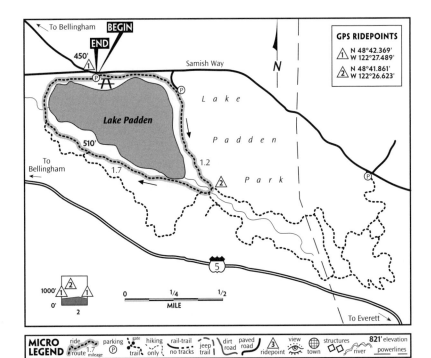

The Ride

The trail runs between the parking area and the lake. Turn left and ride east on the wide, level, dirt trail. The trail winds along the edge of the lake, wrapping behind some playfields. At **1.2** miles, reach a four-way intersection at the eastern end of Lake Padden. Take a hard right, following the lakeshore back to the west. From here, the trail enters a heavily wooded area. At **1.3** miles, ignore a trail up to the left. The trail rolls easily, then climbs a short hill to a fork at the **1.9**-mile mark: Bear right. When you reach another fork, bear right again and descend for a short distance. At the western end of the lake, cross over Padden Creek. From here, continue bearing to the right until you return to the parking area to complete the loop, **2.9** miles.

Gazetteer

Nearby camping: Larrabee State Park
Nearest food, drink, services: Bellingham

52 Upper Lake Padden
☸☸☸

Distance	5.9 miles
Ride	Loop; singletrack, trail
Duration	1 to 2 hours
Travel time	Bellingham—15 minutes; Seattle—2 hours
Hill factor	Some steep sections, some hiking; 470-foot gain
Skill level	Advanced
Season	Late spring, summer, fall
Maps	North Cascades Institute: Bellingham Greenways; Happy Trails: Chuckanut Mountain
Users	Bicyclists, equestrians, hikers
More info	Bellingham Parks and Recreation, 360-676-6985

Prelude

The Lake Padden Park trail system is heavily used by walkers, runners, equestrians, and bicyclists. According to etiquette, as well as common sense, bicyclists should yield the trail to all other users. Don't be a trail bully, or nice, easily accessible areas like this will be closed. If you don't want to deal with the crowds and you'd like to ride more than six miles, go get lost up at Galbraith (Lookout Mountain, Ride 50) or Chuckanut Mountain (Ride 53). But for a quick after-work ride, this is a good choice, with just enough twists, winds, and hike-a-biking to keep it interesting. Take it easy, even on the steep, nasty sections that make this an advanced-skill-level ride.

To Get There

Take Interstate 5 northbound to exit 246, about 15 miles north of Mount Vernon. Start your odometer at the end of the interstate ramp, then turn left on Samish Way toward Lake Padden. At 1.4 miles, pass the Upper Lake Padden trailhead parking area on the left. At 2.6 miles, pass the east entrance to Lake Padden Park on the left. At 3 miles, turn left into the west entrance of Lake Padden Park.

The Ride

Find the trail that runs between the parking area and the lake. Turn left and ride east along the edge of the lake, wrapping behind some play-fields. At **1.2** miles, reach an awkward four-way intersection at the eastern end of Lake Padden. Go right, cross the little stream, then immediately turn left. From here, the trail narrows and climbs. Ignore a trail on the right at **1.3** miles. The trail switchbacks steeply up the bank, probably making the next quarter mile a hike-a-bike. Crest the top of the rise at **1.6** miles, launch down for a short stretch, then traverse to a set of power lines. Reach the power lines at **2.1** miles and bear left, climbing under the power lines, then back into the woods. At **2.2** miles, the trail forks. Take a hard right and climb to a T at **2.4** miles. Turn right again; traverse for a short distance before switchbacking steeply up the hillside.

Some of the switchbacks may have to be walked, but when you crest the hill at **2.7** miles, the pain is over. Noodle across the broad summit to a fork at **2.8** miles and bear left. Reach a T at **3** miles and turn left again. The trail rips down a series of twists and turns. At **3.4** miles, reach a T and turn right. When the trail forks at **3.5** miles, turn right again. At **3.6**

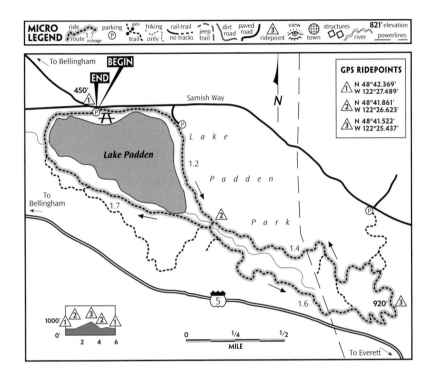

miles, cross under the power lines to the trail beyond (don't turn onto the power-line trail). After another fast stretch (watch out for other trail users), cross over a small stream, then reach the four-way intersection, **4.2** miles. From here, turn left, crossing the stream again, then bear to the right, following the south, more wooded, shore of Lake Padden. Ignore a trail up to the left at **4.3** miles. The trail gently climbs and falls, then climbs to a fork at **4.9** miles: Bear right. When you reach another fork, bear right again and descend for a short distance. At the western end of the lake, cross Padden Creek and continue bearing to the right until you return to the parking area to complete the loop, **5.9** miles.

Gazetteer

Nearby camping: Larrabee State Park
Nearest food, drink, services: Bellingham

53 Chuckanut Mountain

◷◷◷

Distance	12.9 miles
Ride	Loop; singletrack, doubletrack, rail-trail, dirt road; views
Duration	2 to 4 hours
Travel time	Bellingham—15 minutes; Seattle—2 hours
Hill factor	Steep climbs, some hike-a-biking, walking; 1,540-foot gain
Skill level	Advanced
Season	Year-round
Maps	North Cascades Institute: Bellingham Greenways; Happy Trails: Chuckanut Mountain
Users	Bicyclists, equestrians, hikers
More info	Whatcom County Parks, 360-733-2900

Prelude

Rocky cliffs and strange, radical topography make Chuckanut Mountain a unique experience. Some of the climbs are fierce, and in spots the ridge riding is just plain dangerous. The last time I traversed this loop, we thankfully finished riding the ridge before it got completely dark; our lights didn't dim out until the last few switchbacks down Fragrance Lake

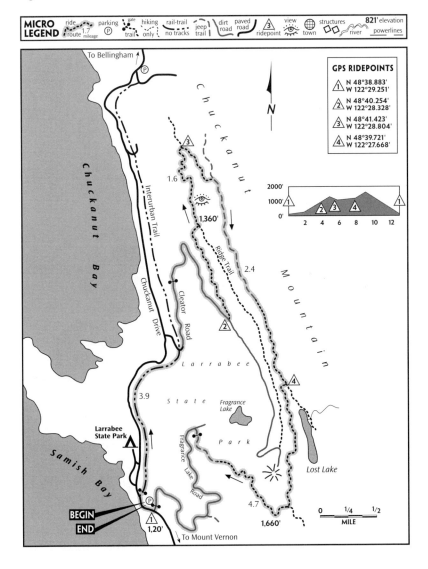

Road. Many more trails crisscross the mountain and more are planned, so the exploration potential is high. Bikes are not allowed on some of the trails on the mountain: Respect those closures. Located just south of Bellingham, Chuckanut Mountain is a hodgepodge of ownership, with Washington State Parks, Whatcom County Parks, Department of Natural Resources, State Department of Wildlife, and the City of Bellingham all having a hand in the management.

To Get There

Take Interstate 5 northbound to exit 246, about 15 miles north of Mount Vernon. Start your odometer at the end of the interstate ramp, then turn right on Samish Way toward Lake Samish. Samish Way bears to the right and crosses over I-5. At 0.3 mile, take the first right onto Old Samish Road. Old Samish Road becomes Lake Samish Road and then ends at a T at 5.1 miles. At the T, turn left on Chuckanut Drive. At 5.2 miles, pass the parking area for the Interurban Trail on the left. At 9.6 miles, pass the southern end of the Interurban Trail on the left. At 9.7 miles, turn left into the large Larrabee State Park parking area.

The Ride

Beginning from the entrance to Larrabee State Park parking area, turn right on Chuckanut Drive and pedal north. After a couple hundred yards, turn right onto the Interurban Trail, a wide, flat, dirt rail-trail. The trail crosses a paved road at **1** mile. At **1.7** miles, the trail drops down into a draw, then climbs back out. At the next road crossing, **1.9** miles, turn right onto Cleator Road, which immediately becomes gravel. From here, the road bends to the left and climbs steeply up the western flank of Chuckanut Mountain. At **2.5** miles, ride through a white gate, and continue the strenuous climb. The road switchbacks to the right, but the grade doesn't subside. Gaps in the trees afford occasional views to the west across Bellingham Bay to the San Juan Islands.

At **3.8** miles, take a hard left turn onto a singletrack. WHOA! This is an easy turn to miss. The trail heads north, traversing through a hemlock and alder forest. After several moderate climbs, reach a T at **4.7** miles, just below the sharp edge of the ridge. Turn left and continue riding north on this ridge-top trail. Much more technical than the previous trail, the ridge-top trail skips along the sheer edge of a high cliff, offering views of the Chuckanut Mountain ridge to the east, Lookout Mountain beyond to the east, and Bellingham to the north. **WHOA!** In several places, the trail comes dangerously close to the cliffs, and walking is recommended. From the cliffs, the rocky, root-strewn trail drops quickly to a fork at **5.4** miles. Take the right fork, shoulder your bike, and hike down a steep slope to the creek, about one-quarter mile. Across the creek, reach a T at a doubletrack and turn right, **5.7** miles.

Pedal up the doubletrack, which is steep in spots, ignoring several trails on the left. At **6.5** miles, the doubletrack becomes a narrow trail. The trail, muddy in sections, winds along the foot of the cliffs (the ridgetop trail is straight above). At **7.8** miles, reach a fork and bear left toward Lost Lake. At **8** miles, arrive at the lake. After hanging out by the lake and checking out the nearby falls, turn around and ride back to the previous fork, now **8.2** miles. Take the trail on the left and head toward Fragrance Lake Road. The trail traverses for a short distance, then ascends at a rapid rate. Some walking may be necessary. When the trail divides at **9.3** miles, bear right and continue climbing toward Fragrance Lake Road. Coast over the top at **9.4** miles. From here, the trail zips down the western slope of Chuckanut Mountain. After a great descent, steer around a gate and reach a T at **10.6** miles. Turn left onto Fragrance Lake Road and start down a fast, dirt-road descent. The road forks at **11.8** miles: Bear right and continue down. At **12.9** miles, reach the Larrabee State Park parking area on the right to complete the ride.

Gazetteer

Nearby camping: Larrabee State Park
Nearest food, drink, services: Bellingham

BELLINGHAM

54 Interurban Trail

Distance	8.6 miles
Ride	Out & Back; rail-trail
Duration	1 to 2 hours
Travel time	Bellingham—15 minutes; Seattle—2 hours
Hill factor	Nearly flat, a couple short hills; 160-foot gain
Skill level	Beginner
Season	Year-round
Maps	North Cascades Institute: Bellingham Greenways; Happy Trails: Chuckanut Mountain
Users	Bicyclists, equestrians, hikers
More info	Bellingham Parks and Recreation, 360-676-6985

Autumn on the Interurban Trail

Prelude

Popular and heavily used, this wide, easy, mostly flat rail-trail traverses a narrow shoulder on Chuckanut Mountain's western flank. In the late afternoon, Bellingham Bay shimmers through the huge maples that provide a shaded canopy. No technical riding ability or conditioning is needed.

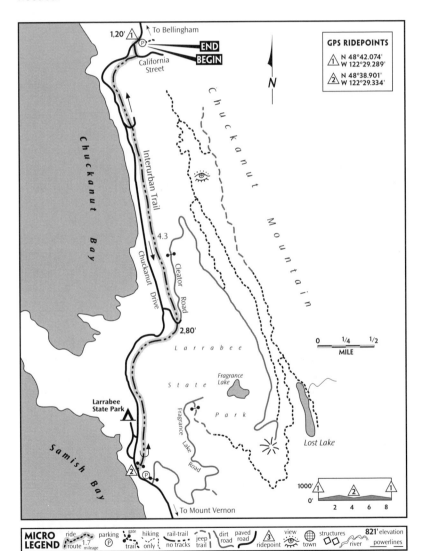

To Get There

Take Interstate 5 northbound to exit 246, about 15 miles north of Mount Vernon. Start your odometer at the end of the interstate ramp, then turn right on Samish Way toward Lake Samish. Samish Way bears to the right and crosses over I-5. At 0.3 mile, take the first right onto Old Samish Road. Old Samish Road becomes Lake Samish Road and then ends at a T at 5.1 miles. At the T, turn left on Chuckanut Drive. Almost immediately, at 5.2 miles, turn left into the gravel parking area: Teddy Bear Cove/Interurban trailhead.

The Ride

From Teddy Bear Cove/Interurban trailhead, pedal out to Chuckanut Drive. Turn left on Chuckanut Drive, then immediately take another left turn onto California Street. Ride up this steep, paved road (this is the only difficult part of the entire trail). At **0.2** mile, turn right onto the Interurban Trail, a wide dirt rail-trail. The trail runs level as it bends around the sheer northern edge of Chuckanut Mountain. At **0.8** mile, cross a paved road. From here, the trail heads due south, paralleling Chuckanut Drive. At **2.5** miles, the trail crosses a paved road, drops steeply into a draw, then climbs back out less than one-quarter mile later. Cross another paved road at **3.4** miles. The trail ends at Chuckanut Drive, **4.3** miles. Turn around here and pedal back to the trailhead to complete the ride, **8.6** miles.

Option

You may want to explore Larrabee State Park and the beach. From the end of the trail at Chuckanut Drive, 4.3 miles, turn right on Chuckanut Drive and then immediately left into Larrabee State Park. **WHOA!** Be extremely careful crossing Chuckanut Drive. From the park entrance, coast down into the park and explore.

Gazetteer

Nearby camping: Larrabee State Park
Nearest food, drink, services: Bellingham

55

WHIDBEY ISLAND

Fort Ebey State Park

✿✿✿

Distance	5.8 miles
Ride	Loop; singletrack
Duration	1 to 2 hours
Travel time	Bellingham—1.5 hours; Seattle—2 hours
Hill factor	Rolling, some steeper climbs; 220-foot gain
Skill level	Intermediate
Season	Spring, summer, fall
Maps	USGS: Port Townsend North
Users	Bicyclists, equestrians, hikers
More info	Fort Ebey State Park, 360-678-4636

Prelude

The maze of trails to the east of Fort Ebey State Park campground traverse both State Park and State Department of Natural Resources property. Some of the trails are narrow, technical, and steep, while others are wide, smooth, and flat—the transitions between trails come quickly and erratically. Many riders will want to chuck the loop described here and explore for several hours. And exploring the crisscrossing trails is really the fun of a ride at Fort Ebey. All of the trails twist and wind through a small area bounded by the campground to the west and State Route 20

to the east, so even if you do abandon this sample ride, you can't get too lost. On summer weekends, some of the trails are heavily used by walkers from the campground, so pay attention.

To Get There

From the town of Oak Harbor on Whidbey Island, travel south on State Route 20. Drive just over 6 miles, then turn right on Libbey Road, following the signs to Fort Ebey State Park. After 1 mile, turn left on Hill Valley Drive. After 1 more mile, reach the Fort Ebey entrance booth. Just beyond the booth, turn left, following the signs to the gun battery. When the road forks, turn right (the campground is to the left). Park at the gun battery parking area.

The Ride

From the parking area at the gun battery, take the paved road back toward the campground. At **0.1** mile, turn right and head for the campground. Coast around the campground loop. Find a trail between campsites 27 and 28, **0.4** mile, and take it. Ignore a wide trail on the right, and ride into the thick woods. Reach a fork at **0.6** mile and bear right on Campground Trail. At **0.7** mile, reach a fork and turn right on Forest Run. When the trail divides at **1** mile, stay to the left. Cross a gravel road at **1.1** miles. After a short, steep hill, **1.4** miles, reach a T under a set of power lines—go right. Almost immediately the trail forks again: Bear right. The trail widens and becomes a doubletrack through a recent timber harvest. Pass by a heap of slash; stay on the main trail, climbing slightly. At **2.1** miles, reach a four-way intersection and turn left. From here, the ragged doubletrack drops and re-enters the woods, becoming a singletrack once more.

After a short technical section, reach a T at **2.5** miles and turn right. In quick succession, bear right and then bear left on Rusty Well, and climb a short hill. At **2.6** miles, reach a fork and bear left. A few pedal rotations farther, bear right on Salal Run, then quickly bear left. Descend a narrow singletrack through a nice forest to a T at **2.75** miles: Turn left. At **2.8** miles, reach a fork and bear left. After two more turns of the crank, arrive at a four-way intersection: Turn right onto Fern Grove. When the trail forks, **2.9** miles, bear left and descend Junk Yard Alley. Reach a five-way intersection, **3.1** miles, turn left on Mainline, and begin climbing a wide trail. At **3.2** miles, take the far right-hand fork. At **3.4** miles, reach an awkward five-way intersection—take the second right. Almost immediately,

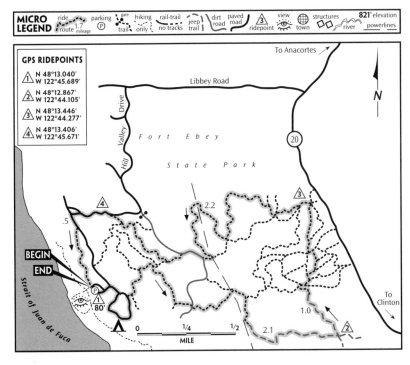

MICRO LEGEND ride route parking gate hiking trail only rail-trail no tracks jeep trail dirt road paved road 3 ridepoint view town structures river 821' elevation powerlines

GPS RIDEPOINTS

⚠1 N 48°13.040' W 122°45.689'

⚠2 N 48°12.867' W 122°44.105'

⚠3 N 48°13.446' W 122°44.277'

⚠4 N 48°13.406' W 122°45.671'

To Anacortes

Libbey Road

N

Valley Drive

Hill

F o r t   E b e y

S t a t e   P a r k

20

4

2.2

3

.5

BEGIN

END

Strait of Juan de Fuca

P 1 80'

0   1/4   1/2   MILE

2.1

1.0

2

To Clinton

this wide trail divides: Bear left and climb the short, steep hill. Stay on the main trail, ignoring several trails on the left.

At **3.9** miles, reach a T and turn right. When the trail forks, bear right again. At **4.2** miles, pass under a set of power lines, ignoring the powerline trail on the left. The trail weaves back to the power lines, then cuts away from them. At **4.5** miles, reach the power lines yet again and turn right. At **4.6** miles, reach an ancient paved road and turn right. Turn left onto a trail at **4.7** miles. When the trail forks, bear right. When the trail forks again, **5.1** miles, turn left. When the trail forks yet again, bear right (left is Brave Heart). Reach a paved road at **5.3** miles and turn left. Coast down past the Fort Ebey State Park entrance booth. At **5.5** miles, turn left toward the campground and gun battery. Just beyond this turn, take the trail on the right. This smooth, wide dirt trail climbs to the parking area at the gun battery to complete the loop, **5.8** miles.

Gazetteer

Nearby camping: Fort Ebey State Park
Nearest food, drink, services: Coupeville, Oak Harbor

56 Heart Lake

◎◎◎

Distance	4.1 miles
Ride	Loop; singletrack, paved road
Duration	1 hour
Travel time	Bellingham—1 hour; Seattle—1.5 hours
Hill factor	Rolling, short hills; 80-foot gain
Skill level	Intermediate
Season	Spring, summer, fall
Maps	Anacortes Community Forest Lands: Trail Guide
Users	Bicyclists, equestrians, hikers
More info	Deception Pass State Park, 360-675-2417

Prelude

Heart Lake is part of Deception Pass State Park, one of the state's busiest parks. However, most of the park's visitors are drawn to the spectacular bridge that spans Fidalgo and Whidbey Islands. Still, on sunny weekends, the trails near Heart Lake can be busy, so watch for other trail users.

Twisty trail near Heart Lake

Rated three wheels because of several technical sections of the trail, this short loop provides a glimpse of the larger trail system in the area. Many riders will want to combine this with Whistle Lake (Ride 58), which begins from the same trailhead.

To Get There

From Interstate 5 near Burlington, take State Route 20 west toward Anacortes. When SR 20 divides, turn left (south) toward Whidbey Island, and set your odometer to zero. At 1.8 miles, turn right on Campbell Lake Road. At 3.4 miles, turn right on Heart Lake Road. At 5.5 miles, turn left into the Heart Lake parking area.

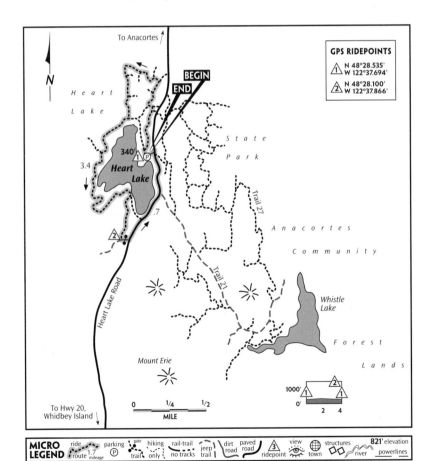

The Ride

As you look toward Heart Lake, find a trail that exits the parking area on the right. The trail immediately forks—turn right onto a narrow single-track, Trail 211. At **0.5** mile, reach a T and turn left. One turn of the pedals farther, reach another T and turn left again. Reach a third T and turn right onto Trail 23. At **0.6** mile, ignore a trail on the left. At **0.7** mile, take Trail 208 on the left (before Trail 23 reaches the road). At **0.8** mile, reach a T, turn left, and cross a stream. When the trail divides at **0.9** mile, bear right, continuing on the winding singletrack, Trail 208.

At **1.2** miles, reach a fork and bear right. Bear right at the next fork a few pedal strokes farther. At **1.4** miles, reach a fork and turn right. At the next fork, bear left. After a few twists in the trail, reach a T at **1.7** miles and turn right. When the trail forks again at **2.4** miles, bear left. At **2.7** miles, pass several trails on the left that spur down to the lake. At **2.9** miles, reach a fork and turn right. At **3.1** miles, arrive at a T and turn left on a wide trail. At the gate, **3.3** miles, take the left fork to Heart Lake Road. Turn left on the road then ride back to the Heart Lake parking area, **4.1** miles, to complete the loop.

Gazetteer

Nearby camping: Deception Pass State Park
Nearest food, drink, services: Anacortes

57 Anacortes Community Forest

⊕⊕⊕

Distance	7.5 miles
Ride	Loop; singletrack, trail
Duration	1 to 2 hours
Travel time	Bellingham—1 hour; Seattle—2 hours
Hill factor	Rolling, short, steep ascents; 320-foot gain
Skill level	Advanced
Season	Spring, summer, fall
Maps	Anacortes Community Forest Lands: Trail Guide
Users	Bicyclists, equestrians, hikers, motorcyclists
More info	City of Anacortes Parks and Recreation, 360-293-1918

Prelude

The City of Anacortes should be commended for purchasing and setting aside the Anacortes Community Forest Lands—it's a recreationalist's paradise just outside of town. They should also be commended for their commitment to shared trails. Be sure to remember this next time you ride here, and be courteous to other trail users. It's a dynamic place, with new trails planned and an active group that oversees and cares for the place, but caring for the place could also mean shutting it down to bicycles if we aren't proper trail stewards. A few of the trails are closed to bicycles, so don't ride on them; if you enjoy riding here, help out on a trail maintenance day or get involved somehow. The trails through this beautiful second-growth forest vary from wide and easy to narrow and nasty. This loop provides an introduction to the Cranberry Lake–vicinity trails but leaves the full exploration potential of the area untapped. Have fun and ride smart, but if you are feeling like really busting loose, head to Lookout Mountain (Ride 50) instead.

To Get There

Zero out your odometer in Anacortes at the intersection of Commercial Avenue and 12th Street. Drive west on 12th Street toward the San Juan ferry terminal. Twelfth Street becomes Oakes Avenue. At 1.7 miles, turn left on Georgia Avenue. At 1.9 miles, turn right on a gravel road toward Cranberry Lake. At 2.2 miles, reach a dirt parking area alongside the lake.

The Ride

From the parking area at the north end of Cranberry Lake, take the trail that crosses the spillway. The trail, narrow with occasional roots, climbs away from the lake. Pass several trails on the right that are off-limits to bicycles. At **0.6** mile, reach a fork and bear right. A few pedal strokes farther, bear right again. When the trail forks at **0.7** mile, bear right, winding up a root-strewn trail. Ignore a faint trail on the left at **1.1** miles. At **1.2** miles, the trail ends at a paved road—turn right, climbing the hill toward a green water tank. At the water-tank fence, bear left on Trail 104. After a short noodle through the woods, reach a four-way intersection above the southeast point of Cranberry Lake, **1.6** miles: Take an easy right turn onto Trail 107 and immediately drop toward the lake.

Just after crossing a short bridge, reach a fork and turn left on Trail 106. At **1.7** miles, bear to the right on a wide trail, climb a short hill, and

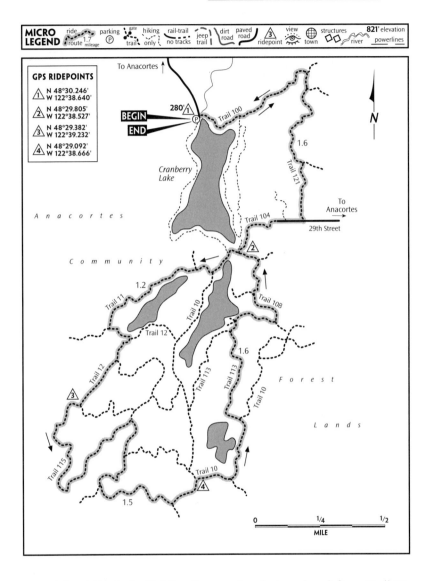

turn right at the fork. At **1.8** miles, reach a fork and go left on Trail 11. When the trail forks at **2.3** miles, bear left on Trail 110. At **2.4** miles, bear right on Trail 12. Ignore Trail 111 on the left at **2.5** miles. Ride to a fork at **2.8** miles and go right on Trail 115. From here, the narrow, winding singletrack climbs steadily, and some walking may be necessary. At **3.5** miles, reach a fork, turn right, and head up the hill. **WHOA!** This is an easy turn to miss. After a difficult climb, reach a fork and bear right on Trail 116. At **3.8** miles, turn left on an unmarked singletrack. The route is twisted and technical.

At **4.1** miles, reach a T and turn left. At **4.3** miles, reach another T and turn right onto Trail 10. Bypass a trail on the right at **4.5** miles. At **4.6** miles, turn left on Trail 113. At **4.9** miles, reach a fork and turn right. Arrive at a four-way intersection, **5** miles, and turn right on Trail 124. At **5.3** miles, reach a T and go left on Trail 108. When the trail divides at **5.5** miles, bear right, continuing on Trail 108. At **5.7** miles, reach a fork and turn left. Ignore a trail on the left. At **5.9** miles, return to the four-way intersection above the southeast point of Cranberry Lake: Turn right on Trail 104 and noodle back to the water tank. Bear right at the tank, ride down the road, and turn left onto Trail 121. From here, continue bearing left as you wind back to the parking area at the northwest corner of Cranberry Lake to complete the loop, **7.5** miles.

Gazetteer

Nearby camping: Deception Pass State Park
Nearest food, drink, services: Anacortes

58 Whistle Lake

⚙⚙⚙

Distance	5.6 miles
Ride	Loop; singletrack, dirt road
Duration	1 to 2 hours
Travel time	Bellingham—1 hour; Seattle—1.5 hours
Hill factor	Steep climbing, hike-a-biking, walking; 580-foot gain
Skill level	Advanced
Season	Spring, summer, fall
Maps	Anacortes Community Forest Lands: Trail Guide
Users	Bicyclists, equestrians, hikers
More info	City of Anacortes Parks and Recreation, 360-293-1918

Prelude

The route to Whistle Lake traverses trails in Anacortes Community Forest lands as well as in Heart Lake State Park. Both areas are crisscrossed by an overwhelming maze of trails and old dirt roads, which make route-

Overlook at Whistle Lake

finding difficult—as you'll see from reading the ride description below. Of course, this bodes well for mountain bikers with exploration in mind. The area isn't too large, so it's difficult to get lost for long. Steep terrain makes the trails in the Whistle Lake and Mount Erie areas much more difficult than the trails around Heart Lake or near Cranberry Lake, so plan on some hike-a-biking.

To Get There

From Interstate 5 near Burlington, take State Route 20 west toward Anacortes. When SR 20 divides, turn left (south) toward Whidbey Island, and set your odometer to zero. At 1.8 miles, turn right on Campbell Lake Road. At 3.4 miles, turn right on Heart Lake Road. At 5.5 miles, turn left into the Heart Lake parking area.

The Ride

From the parking area at Heart Lake, ride back out to Heart Lake Road. Cross the paved road to a trail that bears to the right. At **0.1** mile, reach a four-way intersection and turn left, pedaling uphill. At **0.5** mile, reach an awkward four-way intersection: Bear to the right and then to the right again. At **0.6** mile, reach a fork and bear left. When the trail divides at **0.9** mile, go right and begin a steep ascent. Some walking during this stretch may be necessary. Reach a fork at **1** mile and bear right. A short distance farther, reach a T and turn left. At **1.1** miles, ignore a faint trail on the left. At the fork at **1.2** miles, bear left. Reach another fork at **1.5** miles and go left, continuing up. When the trail divides again at **1.6** miles, take the left fork. At **1.7** miles, bear right.

At **1.9** miles, reach a fork and bear left. From here, the trail descends. Reach a fork at **2.1** miles and bear right, continuing the drop. At **2.9** miles, ignore Trail 202 on the right; continue to the left on Trail 27. Reach a T at **3.2** miles and turn right on a wide trail. At **3.4** miles, reach a fork and take a hard left turn onto Trail 203. At **3.5** miles, reach a fork and bear right on Trail 203B. At **3.6** miles, arrive at a T and turn right. Immediately turn right again. At **3.7** miles, stop and check out a scenic Whistle Lake overlook. Continuing, reach a T at **3.8** miles, turn right, and climb the hill. At **3.9** miles, reach a T at Trail 21 and turn left, traversing the slope. A few turns of your crank farther, bypass Trail 202 on the right.

At **4.1** miles, reach a fork and bear right, climbing again. When the trail divides at **4.2** miles, turn left on Trail 207. Descend the short hill,

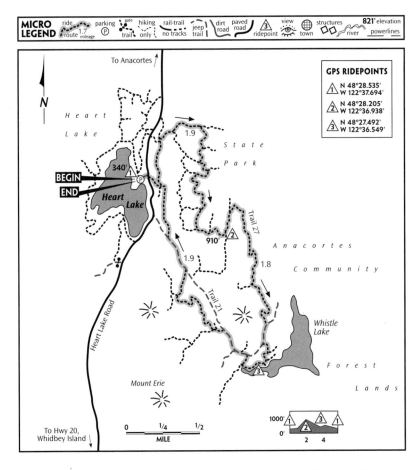

GPS RIDEPOINTS

△1	N 48°28.535' W 122°37.694'
△2	N 48°28.205' W 122°36.938'
△3	N 48°27.492' W 122°36.549'

cross the creek, ignore a trail on the right, then take the second, newer trail on the right at **4.3** miles. After a little walking and some more fast riding, reach a fork, **4.7** miles, and bear right. At **4.9** miles, reach a T at a wide trail: Turn left and descend. At **5.2** miles, reach a fork and turn right onto a lesser trail. From here, descend to a four-way intersection at **5.5** miles. Ride straight through the four-way to reach Heart Lake Road. Carefully cross the road to the parking area to complete the loop, **5.6** miles.

Gazetteer

Nearby camping: Deception Pass State Park
Nearest food, drink, services: Anacortes

Be Responsible for Yourself

The author and publisher of *Mountain Bike! Northwest Washington* disclaim and are in no way responsible or liable for the consequences of using this guide.

1. *Mountain biking is dangerous.* Cyclists can get lost, become injured, or suffer from serious fatigue. The difficulty of the trails described in this guide and the level of skill and experience required to ride safely on the trails are subjective. It is incumbent on each rider to assess his or her preparedness for a trail in light of his or her own skills, experience, fitness, and equipment.

2. *Trail conditions change without notice.* The information contained in this book, as of the date of publication, is as accurate as possible. But conditions on these routes change quickly: Storms, logging activities, stream revisions, landslides, trail construction, and development, among other things, drastically alter trails, in some cases making them dangerous or unridable.

3. *Do not ride on private property.* Some of the rides described in this guide traverse onto private land. Do not conclude that the owner has granted you permission to use the trails listed in this book. Some landowners post signs that allow nonintrusive, daytime use by bicyclists and other users. If the property is not signed, and you are not sure of its status, obtain permission from the owner before riding on the property.

4. *Public jurisdictions may change rules at any time.* Most of the rides described in this guide are located on public land. Although these are currently legal rides, in the future land managers may decide to exclude bicycles, regulate bicycle use, or require permits. Understanding the laws as they change is up to you.

The author and publisher assume absolutely no responsibility for these or any other problems that may occur, nor should they. Hey kids, be responsible for yourselves and the land you are using.